Syntagma of the Evidences of the Christian Religion

Rev. Robert Taylor

THE PUBLISHER TO THE READER.

THOU hast in this Pamphlet all the sufficient evidence, that can be adduced for any piece of history a thousand years old, or to prove an error of a thousand years standing, that such a *person* as Jesus Christ never existed ; but that the earliest Christians meant the words to be nothing more than a personification of the principle of reason, of goodness, or that principle, be it what it may, which may most benefit mankind in the passage through life.

ROBERT TAYLOR.

England, Oakham Jail, May, 1828.

MANIFESTO
OF THE
CHRISTIAN EVIDENCE SOCIETY.
Established Nov. 12th, 1824.

TO ALL PROTESTANTS AND MEMBERS OF PROTESTANT CONGREGATIONS.

MEN AND BRETHREN:

You are hereby invited to attend the Discussions of the Evidences of the Christian Religion, which are held every Tuesday evening, in the Society's Areopagus, 86 Cannon street, City, to which all respectable persons, upon observance of the necessary regulations, are admissible; and where all competent persons, upon a previous notification of their intentions, are allowed to deliver their sentiments upon the topic of discussion.

This Society aims only to promote the love of Truth, the practice of Virtue, and the influence of Universal Benevolence, as opposed to foolish and contradictory systems of religious faith — derived from the ignorance of barbarous ages, and craftily imposed upon the many, for the aggrandisement of the power and influence of a few, who, aware of the suspicious origination of their pretended Divine Revelation, have shown themselves afraid and ashamed to maintain the same, where they might be answered by learned and able men, and might have their accuracy established, or their errors corrected.

Our REVEREND ORATOR, a regular and canonically ordained Clergyman of the Established Church, hath publicly challenged all Ministers and Preachers (and hereby repeats the challenge,) to come forward and show, if they can, the contrary of the FOUR GRAND PROPOSITIONS, which, in the Society's Manifesto, "To all Clergymen, Ministers and Preachers of the Gospel," are declared to have been, as far as to *us* appeared, fully and unanswerably demonstrated.

The PROPOSITIONS are,

I. THAT THE SCRIPTURES OF THE NEW TESTAMENT, WERE NOT WRITTEN BY THE PERSONS WHOSE NAMES THEY BEAR.

II. THAT THEY DID NOT APPEAR IN THE TIMES TO WHICH THEY REFER.

III. THAT THE PERSONS, OF WHOM THEY TREAT, NEVER EXISTED.

IV. THAT THE EVENTS WHICH THEY RELATE, NEVER HAPPENED.

Of these Propositions, the PROOFS are,

I. *That the Scriptures of the N. T. were not,* &c. — Because it *cannot* be shown, by *any* evidence, that they were "written by the persons whose names they bear;" and because it *can* be shown by evidence, both *external* and *internal*, that they were written by *other* persons. — *By evidence external,* In the formal acts and edicts of Christian Emperors, Bishops and Councils, issued from time to time for the general alteration, or total renovation of these Scriptures according to their own caprice. (*a*) And in the

---

(*a*) Such were those of the Emperors Constantine and Theodosius, and this of the Emperor Anastasius. "When Messala was consul (that is, in the year of Christ, 506) at Constantinople, by order of the Emperor Anastasius, the Holy Gospels, as being written by illiterate Evangelists, are censured and corrected." *Victor. Tununensis,* an African Bishop, quoted by Lardner, vol. 3, p. 67. See also an ac-

admissions of the most learned Critics and Divines, as to the alterations which these Scriptures have, from time to time, undergone. (*b*) — *By evidence internal,* In the immoral, vicious, and wicked tendency of many passages therein remaining, and by the insertion of others, whose only drift is to enhance the power of Kings and Priests. (*c*)

II. *That they did not appear, in the times to which they refer,* is demonstrable, — *By evidence external,* In the express admissions of Ecclesiastical Historians, of their utter inability to show WHEN, or WHERE, or BY WHOM, this collection of writings was first made. (*d*) And in the admissions of the most learned critics, as to the infinitely suspicious origination of the present Received Text. (*e*) —

---

count of a general alteration of these Scriptures, "*to accommodate them to the faith of the orthodoxy,*" by Lafranc, Archbishop of Canterbury, as recorded by Beausobre, *Histoire du Manicheisme,* vol. 1, p. 343.

(*b*) ADMISSIONS OF THE MOST LEARNED CRITICS. — 1st. "There were in the MSS of the N. T. *one hundred and thirty thousand* various readings." Unitar. New Version, p. 22. — 2d. "The Manuscripts from which the received text was taken, were stolen by the librarian, and sold to a sky-rocket maker, in the year 1749." Herbert Marsh, Bishop of Peterborough, vol. 2, p. 441. — 3d. For the *most important passage* in the book of Revelation, there was no original Greek at all, but "*Erasmus* wrote it himself in Switzerland, in the year 1516." Bishop Marsh, vol. 1, p. 320.

(*c*) IMMORAL, &c. See Romans iii. 7.; 1 John, ii. 10.; Heb. xii. 29.; Heb. xiii. 17.; Romans, xiii.; 1 Peter, ii. 13.; Luke, xiv. 26, &c., &c.

(*d*) See Mosh. Eccl. Hist., Jones on the Canon, &c., *passim.*

(*e*) RECEIVED TEXT, &c. "The Received Text rests on the authority of no more than twenty or thirty manuscripts, most of which are of little note." Unitar. Version, Introd. 10. "It was completed by the Elzevir edition of 1624." *ib. Mark well!* the retaining therein,

By evidence internal, In innumerable texts therein contained betraying a comparatively *modern* character, referring to circumstances which did not exist till *later* ages, and quoting *other* Scriptures, which had previously formed the faith of the first Christian Churches, but which, without any assignable reason, or alleged authority, have since been rejected. (*f*)

III. *That the persons, of whom they treat, never existed;* Because demoniacs, devils, ghosts, angels, hobgoblins, (*g*) persons who had once been dead, who could walk on water, ride in the air, &c., such as Satan and Jesus Christ, are the persons of whom these Scriptures treat; and that such persons never existed is demonstrable:— 1st. From the utter incongruity of such figments with the immutable laws of sound reason.— 2dly. From the total absence of all historical reference to their existence.— And 3dly. From innumerable passages of these Scriptures themselves, which fully admit the merely visionary Hypostasis of their fabulous hero. (*h*)

---

and circulating as the *Word of God*, with consent or connivance of *all* parties, several passages known and admitted by *all*, to be *Forgeries and Lies.* 1 John, v. 7.; 1 Tim. iii. 16. — *Excellent Morality* this!!

(*f*) COMPARATIVELY MODERN, &c. See 2 John, 9.; 1 Tim. iii. 3.; Ja. v. 14.; Matt. xviii. 17.; 1 Cor. xv. 7, 32.; 1 Pet. iv. 6.

(*g*) HOBGOBLINS. See Acts, xix. 15.

(*h*) VISIONARY HYPOSTASIS. See Luke, ix. 29.; Mark, ix. 2.; Luke, xxiv. 31.; 1 John, v. 6, and innumerable other passages, in perfect accordance with THE TRUE AND GENUINE GOSPELS of the most primitive Christians, which taught that he was ninety-eight miles tall, and twenty-four miles broad; that he was not crucified at all; that he was never born at all; that by faith only are we saved, &c., &c: all equally indicative that Christianity had no evidence at all, but was a matter of mere conceit, fancy, or superstition, from first to last.

IV. *That the events which they relate, never happened,* is demonstrable (further than as a consequence of the preceding proposition) from the fact, that some, many, or all these events, had been previously related of the gods and godesses of Greece and Rome, and more especially of the Indian idol, CHRISHNA, whose religion, with less alteration than time and translations have made in the Jewish Scriptures, may be traced in every dogma and every ceremony of the Evangelical Mythology.

MEN AND BRETHREN:

If these things can be *denied* or *disproved*, your Ministers and Preachers are earnestly called on to do so. Your Missionaries, who boast their readiness to carry their Gospel to the remotest shores of the earth, are again and again *entreated* to become its advocates before assemblies of intelligent and learned men, here, in their native land; where, upon due notice of their intentions, and upon the condition of allowing themselves to be respectfully questioned, and learnedly replied to, they will be received with honor and heard with attention.

By the assembled Society,
ROBERT TAYLOR, A. B. and M. R. C. S.
Orator of the Areopagus, and Chaplain of the Society of Universal Benevolence.

Areopagus of the Christian Evidence Society,
London, February, 1827.

PROLEGOMENA.

To the readers of the Manifesto of the Christian Evidence Society, being, as I hope they are, readers also of the Answer to that Manifesto.

READERS:

Observe ye, I call ye not " MY readers," " my friends," " my intelligent countrymen," " my worthy countrymen," " my intelligent and reflecting readers," "judicious inquirers," &c. Neither do I appeal to you " as men of sense," " as upright men," nor by any of those coaxing and wheedling epithets, which the Rev. Dr. John Pye Smith, the learned and reverend author of the Answer to the Manifesto, gives with such a prodigal liberality, to any body that will have the goodness to see things just as he does, and come to the conclusions which he prescribes. Because I have ever thought that when men appeal to the judgment of the public, it is but fair that they should allow the public to be none the less judicious, intelligent, and upright, even should the verdict of public opinion be decidedly against them. Neither do I take upon myself to tell you, as the Reverend Doctor John Pye Smith does, that if his arguments seem more convincing to your minds than mine, " you must be incapable of reasoning, and immovable by evidence; or, more awfully still, you must have sacrificed both reason and conscience to the darkest depravity of soul," (page 54,) or be no better, than he quotes the authority of the prince of the classical critics, DR. BENTLEY, for calling you " obstinate and untractable wretches;" (page 27.) Because such language, quite proper and evangelical as it may seem to be, when used by doctors of divinity, would in my use of the like, seem to be *blustering*, and, perhaps, justify the doctor in charging me with putting forth my opinions " with a front of unblushing assurance," which, indeed, I should be sorry to do. For if my opinions will not stand upon their own merits, nor get possession of the convictions of those to whom they are submitted, by their own intrinsic demonstration, I have nothing more to say for them; I can neither coax nor frighten the reader to make him show them any sort of favor. I do, indeed, most cheerfully come to the ground of fair and legitimate controversy, and I call on the readers of both sides, as heartily and sincerely as my reverend opponent can, to " think for themselves, to examine fully, reason fairly, and conclude honestly." Only, I cannot go with the doctor, to the length of requesting them to do so DEVOUTLY; " *because the greatness of the occasion demands their* PRAYERS," (p. 55.) No! no! He's welcome to all the advantage the *devotion* and *prayers* can give to *his* side of the argument. I shall never own that mine is in a GOD HELP IT! condition. Not that I mean to blame the doctor for bringing heaven and earth together to make the best of his argument; nor do I think it at all discreditable to any man's moral character, who believes in the efficacy of prayer; that he should turn his thoughts thereto, and feel it to be high time to seek his peace with God upon arriving at the last paragraph of a treatise, in every page of which he had abused God's creature and violated every precept of meekness, forbearance and charity, which he professes to believe that God's authority had bound him to obey.

Now, let the reader, christian or unchristian, partial or

impartial, judicious or injudicious, take the Reply to a Paper entitled, Manifesto of the Christian Evidence Society, into his hand, and before one single argument or objection is advanced against the Manifesto, he finds the reverend answerer almost apoplectic with rage, and choking in the eructations of his own bile. He is in the ridiculous plight of one, who, in the intensity of his passion, forgets his reason and exposes himself to the sufficient refutation of all he has to say, in a HEY DAY! *What's the matter now! What is it all about!*

This, I hold to be as good an answer, and as complete a reproof for the abusive language of this treatise, as the reader will require from me. But to save trouble and to clear the way for genuine and rational argument, in which anger should have no authority, and abuse no weight, I separate the mere epithets of anger and abuse, to stand in a vocabulary by themselves, that the reader may see a fair specimen of the *Christian* spirit and lay it on, or take it off, as he pleases. He will only recollect that he will find nothing of the kind retorted upon the learned, pious and excellent divine, whose disposition prompted as (perhaps we shall see) his argument required them.

VOCABULARY OF EPITHETS applied by the REV. JOHN PYE SMITH, D. D., in vindication of the Christian Instruction Society *versus* the Christian Evidence Society:

Page.
5 — 1. Flagrant instance.
    2. Audacious falsehood.
    3. Not possible to entertain a hope that the person is sincere.
    4. A dishonest man.

PROLEGOMENA.

Page.

- 5 — 5. A false witness.
  - 6. A wilful deceiver.
- 6 — 7. Unhappy writer.
- 7 — 8. Most shameful misrepresentations.
  - 9. Unblushing falsehoods.
  - 10. A front of dogmatical assurance.*
- 9 — Partly of shameful misrepresentations.
  - Partly of downright falsehoods.
  - Gross untruth.
  - Dishonorably omitted.
- 18 — Unfair.
  - Absurd.
- 19 — Disgraceful ignorance.
  - Shameless perversion.
- 22 — Ignorance.
  - Dishonesty.
- 23 — Falsely pretended to quote.
  - Grossly perverted.
- 27 — Disgusting.
  - Falsehood.
  - Audacity.
  - This Manifesto writer.
  - Base misrepresentations.
- 28 — Dishonestly garbled.
- 31 — Dishonorable.
  - Base.
  - Wicked in soul.
  - How miserably incompetent.
  - How dishonest.
  - How aggravated.

---

* All these epithets are expended on the first three pages of the answer before one single exception is taken to the Manifesto.

PROLEGOMENA.

Page.

31 — Fraudulent, wicked man.
32 — Gross falsehood.
   Impudent forgery.
34 — Unprincipled slanderer and deceiver.
   Dishonorable Manifesto writer.
36 — Highest pitch of daring.
   First born of calumny.
   Defying all truth and justice.
37 — This contemptible writer.
40 — The Manifesto writer, with despite of truth and knowledge.
   One of the most unprincipled and impudent liars that ever opened a mouth, or set pen to paper.
43 — Mass of impudence and misrepresentation, so aggravated, that language has no name strong enough.
   Unspeakable folly and wickedness of his mind.
   The pretence of reference to the learned christian advocates, Mosheim and Jones, is *a most infamous piece of forgery.**
53 — The most false of all that have ever disgraced the use of language.
54 — Impudent falsehood.
   This outrageous and insulting writer.
55 — The boastful Manifesto.
   Its artfulness.
   Its effrontery.
   The imposture.

---

* The good doctor's rage seems to have driven him blind, the reader has only to look at the 3d and 4th propositions of the Manifesto, and he will see that no reference is there made or pretended to be made to Mosheim or Jones.

Page.
55 — The dreadful and unblushing falsehoods.
   The outrages on truth and reason.
   Perfect disregard of argumentative equity.
   Its pitiable writer.
   Unprincipled rant.
   A shameless lie.
60 — Folly or knavery.
   This unhappy man.
   Enormous instance.
   Conscious to himself, that he is constantly contriving and publishing the basest falsehoods.
   Alas! miserable man.
   It is not ignorance, it is not error, that prompts his horrid course.

"There is some soul of good in things evil,
   Would men discerningly but sift it out."

So the reader who has a mind to entertain his imagination by gathering all that may be gathered, even from this unsightly accumulation of abuse, will pick up a much greater quantity of admission than the doctor's argument intended to spare.

When a disputant throws off so violently as well nigh to throw himself and all, and dashes upon accusations so unmeasured as, ere they can be looked upon, he himself seems obliged to recall them — (as here, in the doctor's very first paragraph, where he says, "*the books and passages referred to no such thing as is imputed to them,*" and ere he finishes the period, turns it off with the poor mitigation, that the professed quotations are grossly falsified, whereby the reader who can draw an inference must see that the books and passages referred to, *do* say some such thing as is imputed to them;) — he only shows that his disposition to bring a railing accusation is full of stature, while his ability to stand by that accusation is in its infancy.

Undoubtedly, the man who would offer *that* to the public as a professed quotation, for which there really was no original, and *no such thing* in the author, must make a very frightful compromise of his own moral character; and if no probable plea of error, mistake, misprint, or variation of copies could be put in, in arrest of censure, might deserve some one (but one would do) of those sentences of condemnation that flow so copiously from the doctor's pen. But if it really turns out, that the professed quotations are *bona fide* quotations, and the passages referred to are really *there*, in the books and places referred to, I hope a man may be accounted as far from being a "dishonest man, a false witness, or a wilful deceiver," as Dr. Smith himself, even though he may not have seen the passage with Dr. Smith's eyes, nor understood it with his understanding. When charges brought against an adversary are utterly incompatible with each other, their juxta-position is their sufficient refutation; and, like similar terms on the opposite sides of an equation, they may be both effaced, and leave the accuracy of our conclusion unendangered. Thus, when the doctor charges the writer of the Manifesto with "*falsely pretending to quote*," and immediately subjoins "*the tendency and application of which he has so grossly perverted*," (p. 23,) the two charges involve a negation of each other, and constitute an instance of that over-hurling rage, which has to recall its own bolt. "Falsely pretending to quote" (the reader will observe,) is the doctor's *first* fling — but conscious, that 'tis an overfling, he shrinks immediately from the DEFENCE-DIRECT, by which such a charge might be met with — the demonstrative. THERE THE BOOK IS! THERE IS THE PLACE REFERRED TO, — THE PAGE, THE CHAPTER, THE VERSE, THE LINE, THE VERY WORDS; IS IT NOT SO? and you have instead, the doctor's mere opinion, that, the quoter " has grossly perverted the *tendency* and *application* of it:" — upon which tendency and application the doctor may quibble as long as he lists, but his very doing so is an admission that the quoter really HAS quoted, and has NOT "*falsely pretended to quote,*" but has been falsely charged with having done so. For which, I hope, the doctor will see, that "*the greatness of the occasion demands his* PRAYERS." (p. 55.)

When, in the very torrent of abuse, and in the deluge of scornful and contemptuous invective, we discover indications of fear, and that our man of mettle, amidst all his blustering, is only " whistling aloud to keep his courage up," and crying, WHO'S AFRAID? while his heart is in his shoes; we learn that it is not in what is *said*, that we are to look for what is *meant;* and that the *contempt*, that a man expresses for his adversary, is not the gage of his adversary's strength; but of his own weakness. There is no common place in the world perhaps, more than *that* from the Ars Poetica of Horace,—

> " Nec deus intorsit nisi dignus vindice nodus
> Inciderit."

i. e. A man should not disturb the order of nature to help him to look for the cat. Had this learned and *truly Christian* Divine really felt that the Manifesto writer was that *pitiable* writer, that *contemptible* writer, that *miserable, incompetent*, that *disgracefully ignorant* writer, that it was only necessary to refer to the books he had *falsely pretended to quote*, to convict him of *impudent forgeries* and *downright lies :* and that his own Christian *friends*, his intelligent countrymen, his " Judicious Readers," would inevitably think as ill of the Manifesto and its author, as himself: what occasion for this excess of bitterness,— this forestalling denunciation, and anticipative *threat*, to those dear and impartial readers themselves,— that if they shall not decide as he has decided for them, they shall come in for *their* share of his maledictions — *they* also shall be accused of " the darkest depravity of soul," (p. 54.) *they* also shall be held to have sacrificed their reason, violated their duty, and made themselves willing dupes: (p. 55.) and above all, what occasion for doing the thing Devoutly? for calling in the Supreme Being — Divine assistance, Almighty aid, and Infinite wisdom, to answer the arguments of the Manifesto? and thus, after all his railing, to pay me a compliment, o'erfeasting the appetite of vanity itself, and virtually telling his readers all that I could have wished to tell them; and that is, that if they exercise only their own *natural* sense and shrewdness, they will see that there is a greater weight of argument in the Manifesto, than Dr. Pye Smith intended that they *should* see, and that while his sixty pages abound in the language of divine inspiration, grace, holiness, and barbarity: our one — has Reason in it.

Another advantage to be sifted out, from the characteristic style of this reverend divine, is the unintended, but not less effectual, support that it supplies to a position which I have steadily maintained, the irresistible conviction of which first induced me to renounce the Christian faith, the impregnable strength of which still fortifies my mind in that renunciation; and which, when it can, by evidence of history, fact, or reason, be conquered from me, I will, as when the capitol is captured, no longer contend for the borders, and outskirts of a conquered empire. That position is that the influence of Christianity, on the human mind is altogether a BAD and VITIATING influence, that it hardens men's hearts, stupifies their understandings, and vandalizes their manners; that it corrupts nature's sweet juices in them, and turns the milk of human kindness to gall and aconite.

Had there been in this whole treatise, published, as it purports to be, by the Society for Promoting Christian Instruction, and publicly applauded by the Rev. Mr. Blackburn, minister of Claremont Chapel, as having shown the author of the Manifesto to be so great a ——— that none who knew him, would any longer take his word in social life, — had there been, but, per accident, one syllable of decent courtesy, some particle of *mercy*, to have shown itself in the choice of some other, rather then the harshest phrase; or some remembrance of *justice* and fairness, to have admitted the possibility of error and mistake, rather than to have called, what might prove to be no more than error and mistake — "unblushing falsehoods and impudent forgeries:" — the reader might be deceived, as men are, when they read here and there a few scattered precepts of forbearance, meekness, and charity, in the New Testament, into a mistake, as to its essentially ferocious, barbarous, and cruel character: or as children, when they see the polish and the gilding on the sword blade, cease to be aware, that for all the inscriptions it may bear, it is an instrument forged in meditations of cruelty, and destined to works of destruction. But Dr. John Pye Smith is an *honest* Christian: his, is the divinity of the tomahawk and the scalping knife; and the ferocity of his faith, in the Lord Jesus Christ, destroys in him the faculty of being civil. No one can read his treatise, and not read what the tempers and dispositions are which Christianity produces in its most evangelical and distinguished professors, — "O my soul, come not thou into their secret; and unto their assembly, mine honor, be not thou united: their anger is fierce, and their wrath is cruel?"— GENESIS xlix. 6.

But another, the greatest and all-involving "Soul of Good," resulting even from the redundancy of bitterness, that overflows from this, the best answer to the Manifesto of the Christian Evidence Society that the whole challenged Christian community could produce, is, its own admissions. Take every thing that the Reverend Dr. JOHN PYE SMITH has asserted, to be absolutely true; take every thing contained in the Manifesto at all contrary thereto, to be absolutely false; take all the angry epithets he applies to the author of the Manifesto, to be justly due; take all that he assumes to himself, of superior character, talent, learning, ability, veracity; all his vanity can claim, or flattery can give, to be no more than due: and so, even so, the mighty effect the Manifesto aimed at, is yet achieved: and hundreds, who would never have renounced the Christian faith, in consequence of *my attack* upon it, will do so in consequence of the Rev. Dr. Smith's *defence of it*. Our war has been that of Ulysses rather than of Ajax; we have won by our stratagem that which would never have been surrendered to our power. Their ADMISSIONS — their own ADMISSIONS slay them: they admit so much, that nothing is left to be defended, or that is worth defending: the roof of the house, and the foundation of the house, and the four walls, and all the doors and windows into the bargain are surrendered — the rest is Christianity — the rest is all that remains of the house that was founded upon a rock.—" *Quod Thebæ cecidere, meum est.*" The Rev. Doctor has done me the good service of circulating my Manifesto,—he has shown his own congregation, what I would have shown them, too; with this mighty advantage, that the access to conviction was open to his argument's entrance, that would have been barred against mine; and with all his *affected* contempt, and *very sincere* dislike, he has raised me to the enviable pre-eminence of the man, who makes those, who hate him, the ministers of his purpose, and the instruments of his power; who does the thing he sought to do by means of their hostility, makes their malice to effectuate his designs, and their rebellion to subserve his will. " This glory, never can his wrath or might extort from me ! "

Whoever shall have read the *admissions*, which the Manifesto of the Christian Evidence Society has wrung from its best and ablest opponent, and trusted himself to see the pretended evidences of Christianity, as being (say *not so bad* as I had represented them, but) *no better* than the Answer to the Manifesto could make them, may be a hypocrite, and so may be a Christian still; but he can no longer be a Believer. Did I not aim at this effect? Have I not maintained that Christianity is *the greatest curse that ever befel the human race*? Have I not laid out my life, and my life's energies, to deliver and emancipate men's minds from the dreadful influence of that curse?

Am I not now a prisoner,—the martyr of this great and glorious cause?

Have I not made every treatise which has been written against me, and every cruelty that has been inflicted on me, more detrimental to the cause of Christianity, than it could be injurious to me? Then rail at me, all ye Doctors of Divinity — Curse me, all ye Priests ; the spell, that subjugated, oppressed, and insulted millions to your tyrannous dynasty is broken :

> "———— Hoary headed selfishness has felt
> Its death blow, and is tottering to the grave:
> A brighter morn awaits the human day;
> War with its million horrors, and fierce hell,
> Shall live but in the memory of time,
> Who, like a penitent libertine shall start,
> Look back, and shudder at his younger years."

SECTION I.

ON THE GENERAL EVIDENCE OF THE PRETENDED GENUINENESS OF THE CHRISTIAN SCRIPTURES.

I SHALL follow the learned and reverend doctor, according to his own method, section for section, page for page. The reader will please to observe, that it is on the eighth page of the Answer to the Manifesto, that he will meet with the very first sentence that purports to be a reply to any part of the Manifesto. And here he will observe, that, what in the Manifesto are called PROPOSITIONS, and which, as *propositions*, are accompanied by subjoined PROOFS, and submitted in public challenge to all ministers and preachers, to come forward and show, if they can, the contrary: those *propositions* being declared to have been, as far as to us appeared, (*i. e.* to the assembled Christian Evidence Society,) "fully and unanswerably demonstrated." These propositions are very conveniently called by the doctor, *assertions*, as if they had not been accompanied by any attempted proof; nor offered in fair and ingenuous challenge of disproof: that so he might bring these *propositions* down to the level of all that he can bring against them — *assertions*, — and seem justified in saying of them, what can only justly be said of *assertions*, that they are uttered with "a front of dogmatical assurance."

We shall find this distinction of some importance.

When EUCLID published to the world his Treatise of Geometry, he put forth what he called *propositions*, he accompanied them with what seemed in him to be *proofs*, and he submitted them in public challenge to all the geometricians in the world, " to come forward and show, if they could, the contrary." Now, just such a geometrician, as Dr. Smith is a divine, would have been the man who might have chosen to call those *propositions*, assertions, to say that they had been put forth " with a front of dogmatical assurance ; " or, that they were sufficiently answered, by applying to the *proposer* of them, any of the abusive and virulent epithets of Dr. Smith's evangelical vocabulary. But calling the two first PROPOSITIONS of the Manifesto, assertions (to wit, 1st., THAT THE SCRIPTURES OF THE NEW TESTAMENT WERE NOT WRITTEN BY THE PERSONS WHOSE NAMES THEY BEAR, and 2nd., THAT THEY DID NOT APPEAR IN THE TIMES TO WHICH THEY REFER ; and, taking the two to be but one,) the doctor (whom nobody must suspect of being dogmatical,) gives what his Homerton College students may consider as a complete refutation of the two first propositions of the Manifesto in the words —

" Our summary reply, to the first of these assertions, is this : We have the *most satisfactory* evidence, that the books of the New Testament WERE written at the time which they intimate, and by the persons to whom they are attributed."—*page 6, Sec. I.*

It is a *summary* reply indeed ! Let the reader digest the knowledge he hath gained ! and perhaps he will see, that it was a good stroke of policy to call the PROPOSITIONS *assertions*, and to complain of the front of dogmatical assurance, with which they had been put forth ; because, by so doing, he might forestall any suspicion of his own dogmatism, while he was making the best of the best materials he had. Pull down the ground about you and you raise yourselves — call PROPOSITIONS accompanied by PROOFS and submitted in challenge of disproof, mere *assertions*, and then when you can do no better, you know you may begin and call ill names, and say that one assertion is as good as another.

"WE have the *most satisfactory* evidence," says this learned, unquestionably most learned, divine. Have you so? and by my honor, I'm glad of it for your sakes; but who are WE? For if in that WE, *I*, and half a dozen whom I could answer for, be included, *I* must remind the doctor that *satisfactory* is not quite the adjective that one man has the right to predicate of another man's meal: and that WE have not the most satisfactory evidence. I deny not, I dispute not the satisfactoriness, the abundance, the crapula, the surfeit of evidence for the divinity of the Christian Scriptures that must appear to the minds of those whom those Scriptures are the means of seating in professional chairs and college dignities, of enabling them to arrogate the more than mortal prerogative of being ambassadors of Omnipotence, of swelling in idle, vain-glorious, and useless pomp, and driving in triumph over the insulted intelligence and ruined fortunes of the starving and deluded people — and only starving because they are deluded.

If, indeed, the genuineness of the Christian Scriptures can be disproved, or, which is the same thing, if the great body of society shall be brought to see (what I will lose no means of showing them,) that those Scriptures really are *not* genuine! Why the Christian craft is up! Doctors of Divinity will become — ah! what will they not become? They will be obliged to turn honest, and so —

Farewell pride, pomp, and circumstance of glorious priestcraft.
And Oh! ye Moorfields pulpits, whose loud throats
Th' immortal Jove's dread clamors counterfeit,
Farewell! The Reverend occupation's gone!

Now, reader, be awake, and see what you see, and see

this reverend doctor of divinity, after having given you his own unqualified and unsupported *assertion* that the evidence for the genuineness of the Christian Scriptures is "*most satisfactory*," and challenged for that assertion that it should, on the ground of his doctorial dignity and autocratical WE, be received as a summary reply to the propositions of the Manifesto: in the very next sentence, receding in his bold advance and leaving ground enough, e'en if there were no more, for the firm footing of the proposition he assails.

"Several of them (that is, of the books of the New Testament,) do not bear any name in the beginning or body of their composition." Say you so, Sir? Then what say common sense and common honesty, upon turning to your English copies of the New Testament, which you are circulating by your Bible Societies, and never ceasing from your pulpits to speak of as a revelation from a God of Truth, and finding that there is not one of those books but what does bear a name in the beginning, the name of some supposed *inspired apostle*, per virtue and authority of which name, and of which alone, it derives all its influence on the minds, all its obligation on the consciencies of men.

If that terrible and heart-appalling summons on the prostration of all minds — the surrender of all the faculties of man — his submission as unto fate — his obedience even unto death — if that dread — THUS SAITH THE LORD! or, *thus by his Holy and Inspired Servant and Messenger hath he said* — turns out at last that THUS he hath not said — but thus hath said — we know not whom — but who had no more right to say so than the Tutor of Homerton College. What is forgery, what is imposture, if this be not? And if this be the predicament of "several" of the books, of which there are but twenty-seven altogether, while we know not *which*, nor *how many* that several may be; what can we say of the man who, with such an admission before him, that imposture has been at work; that *forgery* is there; that the names of *several* of the books which are *prefixed*, were not prefixed by the persons whose names they purport to be; and that a parade of authority is set forth in the translation for which there is no support in the original — what, I ask, can we say of the man who will still persist in ascribing Scriptures of such infinitely suspicious *external* evidence (to say nothing of their incongruous, absurd, and contradictory contents,) to the immediate authority of a God of infinite wisdom, goodness, and truth? What? — But that he had better do it "DEVOUTLY" — he had better do it "with PRAYER," (p, 54) — For he hath need of forgiveness; and perhaps a little CONFESSION, too, might help to disgorge the o'er-cloyed conscience.

But never was the wilely shirking traitor that had turned King's evidence against his brother thieves, beaten by cross-examination into so forlorn a *come-off* as that of our divines, who, after having all along arrogated for the writings of the New Testament — a supernatural and superhuman authority — and held it to be no more than "the words of truth and soberness," to say of *the whole Bible* that "it hath God for its author, happiness for its end, and truth, without any mixture of error, for its matter," at last turn round on us with the startling surrender of every thing, by attempting to show that these writings have as good proofs of their genuineness, or perhaps better, than the works of Thucydides, Xenophon and Demosthenes, among the Greeks; or of Cicero, Cæsar, and Livy, among the Romans — works which have absolutely no authority at all, which never pretended to any, but which do each of them, in very many places, expressly discard and disclaim all pretence to authority, and in all and every part of them offer themselves in submission to the reader's judgment, not in control or direction of it. These writings claim no particle or degree of our admiration on account of their being respectively the works of Thucydides, Xenophon, Demosthenes, Cicero, Cæsar, or Livy, but are esteemed for their intrinsic and indefeasible merit only, which would be and remain the same, neither more nor less, though critical research should discover to the world that it was not Xenophon but Clearchus that wrote the Anabasis; not Demosthenes, but Isocrates that delivered the Olynthiacs; not Cicero but Atticus that composed the De Officiis.

"The thing we call a rose would smell as sweet,
If it were called by any other name,"

but not so your ROSE of SHARON — if that be not in the predicament ye have predicated of it — if it be not that

"Th' etherial spirit o'er its leaves doth move,
And on its top descends the mystic dove,"

Paugh! it's a vile stinking darnel, and hath neither color, scent, or medicine to save it from our loathing!

The "*intelligent*" reader, unless he has a mind to surrender his intelligence, ought not to suffer himself to be coaxed, by being called "*intelligent*," into a *peace* and WELL-A-DAY sort of compromise with this NO-HELPING-IT-NOW condition of divine revelation.

"*The titles at the head of each book were prefixed, not by the authors, but by the early transcribers.*"

But reader, is it of no consequence, where eternity is assumed to be at stake, to ask the obvious question? Who were those early transcribers — and how early?

And wherefore it is, that supposing that those early transcribers had a delegated or vicarious right to affix titles to some of the books, there should be several to which no titles are affixed — not even by those early transcribers?

Observe ye, then, the exact plight of the general evidence for the genuineness of the Christian Scriptures, upon Dr. Smith's own showing.

Of *several* of the twenty-seven books of the New Testament, the doctor not showing *which* nor *how many* those several are, it is admitted that the names they bear were not affixed to them by their authors — no, nor even by their early transcribers. — COROLLARY — By whom, then, were they affixed but by comparatively modern transcribers who could have had no authority, neither direct nor delegated, for what they did?

But, of those books which are not included in the *several*, not saying which they be, but which have the higher authority of having names prefixed to them, not by their authors, but by certain unknown *whom* and unknown *when* early transcribers; *that* circumstance which in any other would be thought a little discouraging, in the doctor's reasoning " *involves a proof of the general belief and notoriety that those books were the genuine productions of the writers whose names were familiarly attached to them.*"

Now, reader, as I at least *wish* to be innocent of " dogmatical assurance," I will only *ask leave* to ask you to ask yourself whether there be not two considerably important *quærenda* for your logic, even from this position, emergent —

1st — Whether the circumstance of titles being prefixed to certain books by persons who were certainly not the authors of them does certainly involve a proof of the general belief and notoriety that those books were really the works of the persons to whom they were so ascribed?

And secondly — Whether the public notoriety and general belief of those early times (supposing ourselves to have competent means of knowing what that public notoriety and general belief was,) would itself be sufficient ground for concluding that those early transcribers, or those who paid them for transcribing *(good honest men,)* could not possibly be less trust-worthy than public notoriety and general belief held them to be — that they were no more capable of intending to deceive the people than the people were of forming too high an opinion of them — that they could not put the wrong name rather than the right one to the title of the matter that they had transcribed — that in those ages, seventeen or eighteen hundred years ago, learning was so generally diffused and public notoriety so sure to find them out, that they could have had no opportunity of doing so even if they had been so inclined — that though God only knows who they were or by what motives they were actuated, yet we may be absolutely sure that when a manuscript would fetch a hundred times the price for bearing the name of JACK rather than of GILL, they were too conscientious and disinterested to be capable of substituting the one for the other?

To solve these important *quærenda*, I could supply the reader with quotations from Ecclesiastical history, Councils, Fathers, &c., as extensively, perhaps, and as fairly as the Professorial Doctor, for indeed, "*it is not ignorance, it is not error, that prompts my horrid course,*" (p. 60)—but if the reader happens to be a member of the CHRISTIAN INSTRUCTION SOCIETY, the chance is that he may have been *instructed* by the precepts as well as by the example of this Christian instructor, to call such quotations a parade of learning and authority and an ostentatious reference, &c., — and when he found the quotations absolutely correct — and *in* the authors — there as quoted, page for page, line for line, word for word, he might like the Rev. Divine, run stark-staring desperate — foreswear his own eyes — and call me " the greatest liar that ever opened a mouth, or set pen to paper," &c., &c. So as I hope he will not apply these epithets to Dr. Smith, however he may seem to contradict himself — himself shall be my authority. Let quotations made by *him* be held to be fairly quoted, and these are his own materials for solving the *quærenda* which arise from his own positions.

" The documents of history for that period and some centuries after, are very obscure. In the time of Simon and the learned Benedictines of St. Maur, very great and numerous errors with respect to the persons and transactions of those dark ages were commonly received," &c. (p. 16.)

" It is well enough known that in the early ages of Christianity, many silly and fraudulent persons composed fictitious narratives of the life and actions of Jesus Christ and his apostles, and gave them out as the writings of Peter, Nicodemus, Thomas, Barnabas, and even Judas Iscariot. By far the larger part of these spurious compositions have long ago dropped into deserved oblivion. That they ever existed, is known only from the records of the early Christian writers, usually called the Fathers, and they were always rejected by the general body of Christians." — (p. 40.)

Reader! is this forgery? Is it I who have said all this? Or will Dr. Smith again charge me with putting forth what I would put forth, with a front of dogmatical assurance; if I only suggest the questions which arise from his own statements, and leave it to himself or to any body in the world who *can* do so, to answer them :—

1. If the documents of history at any given period, and for some centuries after that period are very obscure, what is there to render them such as a man may rest his salvation upon prior to that period?

2. If very great and numerous errors with respect to the persons and transactions of the eleventh century are admitted, what guarantee have we for the infallibility of the first?*

3. Shall our knowledge that a man was infinitely mendacious in his mature life, lead us to infer that his word might be depended on in his infancy?

4. If eleven hundred years (from the 3d or 4th to the 15th or 16th century — from the more than barbarous ignorance, and grosser than pagan superstition which prevailed over the whole Christian world,) are justly called the DARK AGES — how can mankind be said to have been *enlightened* by the Gospel? — The world is surely as forlorn of evidence to prove any beneficial effect of the

---

* Adeo verbum Dei inefficax esse censuerunt, ut regnum Christi sine mendacio, promoveri posse diffiderunt. — *Epist ad Casaubon,* p. 303.

It was a maxim of the Church that it was an act of virtue to deceive and lie, when by that means the interest of the Church might be promoted. — *Mosheim,* vol 1. p. 382.

For if the truth of God hath more abounded through my lie unto his glory, why yet am I also judged as a sinner? — *Romans* iii. 7.

"For notwithstanding those twelve known infallible and faithful judges of controversy (*i. e.* the twelve apostles,) there were as many and as damnable heresies crept in, even in the apostolic age, as in any after age, perhaps, during the same space of time — so little will infallibility serve the turn it is set up for." — *Reeves' Preliminary Discourse to the Commontory of Vincenius Lirinensis,* p. 190.

pretended revelation upon men's *understandings*, as an abusive and scurrilous priest would be if called on to show that it had any influence in softening his temper, or mitigating his virulence.

5. If in the early ages of Christianity, *many* silly and fraudulent persons composed fictitious narratives, &c., must not fictitious-narrative making have been a good trade?

6. Must they not have found the Christian community easily imposed on?

7. How then can Dr. Smith, or any one else, presume to say that they were always rejected by the general body of Christians?

8. Or, who the general body of Christians were?

9. Or, that rejection by the general body of Christians was a sufficient proof that the matter ought to have been rejected?

10. Or, that admission by the general body of Christians was a sufficient proof that the matter ought to have been admitted?

11. Who were the representatives of the general body of Christians that exercised for them the stupendous arbitration?

12. Were there no dissenters from the general body?

13. Will the dissenterian Dr. John Pye Smith maintain that no respect could possibly be due to those dissenters?

14. If by far the larger part of those spurious compositions have long ago dropped into *deserved* oblivion, who is to determine now that that oblivion was deserved?

15. Who is to determine that they were spurious?

16. Who is to determine that those Scriptures which *have* been preserved, (owing their preservation as they do

to those who had the strongest possible interest in undervaluing and decrying them,) are a fair specimen of what the others were?

17. Would not those who wished the received Scriptures to be held in honor make the best of them?

18. Would not those who wished the rejected Scriptures to be held in contempt, make the worst of *them*?

19. If writings were forged in the names of Peter, Nicodemus, Thomas and Barnabas, why might not those which appear under the names of Matthew, Mark, Luke and John, have been forgeries also?

20. Why should not all the rest of the disciples have written gospels, as well as the two, Matthew and John?

21. Why should not the gospels of all the rest of the disciples have had as good a claim on our credence, as those of Matthew and John, who were no more than disciples — and a better claim than those of Mark and Luke, who were no disciples at all?

22. If the gospels which appear under the names of Matthew, Mark, Luke and John, appear infinitely more respectable than those which appear under the names of Peter, Nicodemus, Thomas and Barnabas, is not that circumstance a presumption in favor of the prior existence of those of Peter and Nicodemus, Thomas and Barnabas?

23. Assuming that there had been some real foundation for the gospel story, is it not a presumption — that the more simple, artless, and awkward style of telling it, would have been the original one?

24. If all accounts or narratives of Jesus Christ and his apostles were forgeries, as 'tis admitted that all the apocryphal ones were — what can the superior character of the received gospel prove for them; but that they are merely superiorly executed forgeries?

compositions of no such persons as they are ascribed to.

Let the reader answer these questions to his own convictions! Let him make them his own! and if he should not answer them, as he may perhaps guess that I should, he will yet, I hope, observe that with all my dogmatical assurance and unblushing effrontery, I have not yet assumed the style of my reverend opponent — nor shall I take upon myself either to say or even to think that " he must have sacrificed his reason and conscience to the darkest depravity of soul."

The doctor's avowedly " fearless challenge to produce any writings approaching to the same professed antiquity, whose genuineness is supported by evidence equally abundant and unexceptionable," coupled with the remark which follows it, partakes of his characteristic style; it is the desperaund forlorn flinging off of a man who, when he finds he has nothing reasonable to say, plays *devil may care* as to what he says, and stakes his last throw upon the chance to frighten you from observing the shallow weakness of his argument, by the sonorous insolence of his vituperation.

" *Approaching to the same professed antiquity.*" What! an apology for them — there is wonderful evidence for their genuineness, considering how old they are. But were his challenge to such a comparison accepted, and all the advantage of complete victory (which, by the bye, is infinitely doubtful,) in his hands: What would it prove for the pretensions of divine revelation, to prove that its records stood on as good ground, or probably better, for the chance of being genuine, than the histories, legends, romances, or poems of an equally remote antiquity, which it never mattered one penny or one care to anybody, whether they were genuine or not?

Should we take up Hardoin's hypothesis and persuade ourselves that the classical writings were the

but were dexterously got up by the monks of a much later age than that to which they purport to belong, why, well done the monks! who have done as well as the authors themselves, had they been genuine, could have done! and there's the amount of the mischief.

Suppose it should one day be discovered that the Paradise Lost was written by no such person as John Milton, or that Gibbon's Decline and Fall of the Roman Empire, was no work of Gibbon's; no material question is affected, no important issue is at stake. But as the doctor would find it very hard to name any one celebrated work of antiquity that was ever in such a predicament, that about the time of its appearance, or at any time, there either were or possibly could have been rival and competitive works, affecting to have been written by the same author, and claiming equal merit: — as bold a writer as himself might fearlessly challenge him to show that any one of the writers he has named has not a thousand fold better general evidence than any that can be pretended for the writings of the New Testament, and might even defy imagination itself to imagine how writings which so strong interests, craft, policy, passions, and prejudices of men, had concurred for so great a length of time to impose upon the world as divine oracles, could possibly betray stronger and clearer marks of forgery and imposture than are to be found in these.

Note. — " This opinion has always been in the world, that to settle a certain and assured estimation upon that which is good and true, it is necessary to remove out of the way whatsoever may be an hinderance to it. Neither ought we to wonder that even those of the honest, innocent primitive times made use of these deceits, seeing for a good end they made no scruple to forge whole books."—*Daille on the use of the Fathers*, b. 1, c. 3. Passim occurrunt patrum voces de dæreticis conquerentium, quod fraudum artifices, ut somniis suis autoritatem conciliarent, libros quibus ea in vulgus proseminabant, celleberrimæ cujusque ecclesiæ Doctoris imo et Apostolorum nominibus inscribere ausi essent.—Johannes Dallæus, lib. 1, c. 3.

SECTION II.

OF ACTS AND EDICTS FOR THE ALTERATION OF THE SCRIPTURES.

"Nothing of the kind is to be found in history," says this unassuming and humble-minded divine, and *that*, too, within the echo of his own reproof of another, for having spoken with too much confidence. The greatest historian that ever lived would have been restrained by the modesty that ever accompanies great and substantial knowledge from saying more than, that, in the extent of historical reading, or within his memory of what he had read, he recollected nothing of the kind; a dissenterian Doctor of Divinity may say anything. "It is scarcely possible to imagine a greater untruth than this assertion," says our infallible D. D.! Yes, if being all that it purports to be, a *reference* merely, to direct the reader to the sources where he shall find matter yielding such support as he himself may judge whether it be competent or not to support the proposition which he is called and invited to disprove, be an assertion — and if, being an assertion, it were an *untruth*, it would yet be possible to imagine a grosser one, because it would be possible to imagine a man's attempting to make the world believe that there could be nothing in the whole compass of history but what had come under his observation, and could not escape his memory.

"With respect to Constantine* and Theodosius, the

---

* "*With respect to Constantine*," — *if the reader choses to refer to the life of Constantine, by his intimate friend Eusebius*, (book 4, chap. 36, 37.) The reader is to suspect no gasconade here, no ostentatious pretence of acquaintance with the original Greek of Eusebius, no

writer of the Manifesto has *dishonorably omitted,*" &c. Could there be no supposable reason for *an omission* where the whole matter was intended but as *an index,* and was to be compressed on one single page; but that it must needs be *dishonorable?*

Reader, turn thine eye to page 43, and see what Dr. Smith can plead in excuse for his own sins of omission — where his matter occupies 60 pages. There you will see that he holds it authority sufficient for one of his proposi-

---

concealment of the English translation which he must have found so useful, and no suppression of what — if he had any pretensions to the character of a scholar — he *must have known* of the character of Eusebius, and how little entitled to credit any life of his *intimate friend* and patron must be, written by the courtly bishop, who danced attendance on the tyrant's pleasure in an age when it was an established " Maxim of Christian piety, that it was an act of virtue to deceive and lie, when by such means the interests of the church might be promoted." (Mosheim's Ecc. Hist. London, 1811, vol. 1, p. 382,) and when he himself confesses, or rather avows his own adoption of that pious principle, as the rule of his fidelity as an historian, and takes a pride in himself in having related whatever might redound to the *glory,* and SUPPRESSED all that could tend to the disgrace of religion." Gibbon, vol. 2, p. 490.

Of the power of the Roman emperors, and of all Christian kings, princes, and governors, to alter the text of scripture to any extent they pleased, the proofs are so abundant that their abundance only stood in the way of enumeration. See their innumerable decrees, acts, and edicts to this effect, in every history of their reigns. " The proofs of that supreme power of the emperors in religious matters, appear so incontestible in this controversy that it is amazing it should ever have been called in question." Mosheim, cent. 4, part 2, vol. 1, p. 406, note 9. See the Bible itself. See also the plenary inspiration ascribed to kings in the Liturgy. " O, Almighty God, we are taught by thy holy word that the hearts of kings are in thy rule and governance, and that thou dost dispose and turn them as seemeth best to thy goodly wisdom." See also, the king's title, " OF THE CHURCH ON EARTH, THE SUPREME HEAD."

tions: (to wit — that the OCCASIONS on which the miracles were wrought — exempli-gratia, the occasion of supplying *more wine* to fellows who were half seas over already, the occasion for cursing a fig-tree, the occasion for playing the devil with the pigs, were occasions WORTHY of the interposition of divine omnipotence, a proposition which surely must be as hard to prove as any contained in the Manifesto) — that it " has been shown with an abundance of evidence' by numerous and well-known authors, to whom access is easy. Within the narrow limits of these pages, it is impossible to do justice to the argument; and surely it may be expected that every person who feels the infinite importance of the subject will take the little pains necessary to obtain the requisite information."

Shall these, his own words! this, his own excuse! be good and valid for himself — and it is so: while nothing less than a *dishonorably* intended omission is to be charged on me, for not having defeated my own object — by making my Manifesto too much to be contained in a Manifesto: when the names of CONSTANTINE and THEODOSIUS were *sufficient* to refer any reader to the pages of a work so easy of access as Gibbon's Decline and Fall of the Roman Empire: and when, for the name and instance of the emperor Anastatius, as not being so well known nor to be found in a work so easy of access; I had supplied the reference, which in that more essential case alone seemed necessary, to the author, the volume and the page where it is to be found?

And of this the doctor, after having in the title of this section designated it as *a pretence*, and in the section itself characterized it — as " the grossest untruth that could be imagined;" in the very next section and in the very next page, admits that it is indeed *fairly transcribed* from Dr.

Lardner's translation of it. In that admission, however, thrusting from himself the credit of fairness, which the admission might win for him, by the unfair and unworthy insinuation that — I could not have become acquainted with the passage, but by means of a translation.

How far the piety and conscientiousness of Constantine,* as guaranteed by the historical veracity and impartiality of his intimate friend Eusebius, is positive evidence of the care and diligence which were exercised in making copies of the scriptures; or whether extraordinary " care and diligence in making copies of the scriptures,"

---

* Constantine had a father-in-law whom he impelled to hang himself: he had a brother-in-law whom he ordered to be strangled: he had a nephew of twelve or thirteen years only, whose throat he ordered to be cut: he had a son whom he beheaded; he had a wife whom he ordered to be suffocated in a bath; and so, when he had made a clear house for himself, his mind took a serious turn. But there was nothing in the religion of the ancient paganism, that could give comfort to the conscience of a sinner, — the ancient paganism had no propitiation for throat-cutting, no atonement for child-killing. Its terrible language was,

> Ah nimium faciles, qui tristia crimina cœdis
> Fluminea tolli posse putetis aquâ,
> Non bove mactato cœlestia numina gaudent,
> Sed quæ præstanda est, et sine teste fide.
>   Ovid (*as I remember.*)

O! this would never do for Constantine — here was nothing for a sinner's hope to rest on; but the religion of the Galilean proclaimed that the blood of Jesus Christ cleanseth from all sin, (1 John i. 7,) and Constantine became a Christian. Christianity consequently became the religion of the State, and — " the terrors of a military force silenced the faint and unsupported murmurs of the pagans." Gibbon (*as I remember.*) The exercise of the pagan religion was prohibited under pain of death, by an edict of the emperors Valentinian and Marcian, in the year 451. See the edict of Theodosius, Gibbon, vol. 5, p. 15.

exercised by such pious and conscientious Christians as Constantine and Eusebius — is not itself an extraordinarily suspicious circumstance against the chance of their remaining uncorrupted, — (as sure no man would think a treasure the more likely to remain untouched, for being under the extraordinary care and diligence of a known thief;) or how far Dr. Smith can take upon himself to infer — what could or could not have been "*thought of* by the emperor," are considerations which the reader will determine according to the bent of his own reflections.

I only claim his observance that unmeasured as are the doctor's charges against me, his amount of proofs as yet stands at nought and carry nought.

SECTION III.

ALTERATION OF THE GOSPELS IN THE REIGN OF ANASTASIUS.

"*The passage from Victor, an obscure author who wrote a Chronicle of about twelve pages, of which this sentence is an article, is indeed fairly transcribed from Dr. Lardner's translation of it,*" &c. "*But mark the honesty of this Manifesto writer.*" Well, o' God's name, mark his honesty!

"*He copies the passage which makes for his purpose.*" Well, and what would you have said of him, if he had copied a passage which did *not* make for his purpose?

"*And which he would in all reasonable probability never have known of had not that Christian advocate furnished him with it.*" And how could anybody know of anything if nobody had furnished him with the knowledge of it? or what would the doctor have said if this bit of knowledge had been furnished for me by *an infidel,* or if I had supplied it purely from my own invention?

" *But he says not a syllable of the evidence which was before him in the very same page of the total falsehood of the statement, as it is professed to be understood by some modern infidels.*" But suppose what was before him, seemed to him to be no evidence at all?

I take this clause to comprehend a fair specimen of the doctor's claims to the praise of candor, fairness, and integrity.—His *candor,* in charging it to a want of honesty, that being confined to compress my whole quantum of matter within the border of the Manifesto, I had taken no notice of what I thought did not make for my purpose. — His *fairness* in implying that I had rejected evidence which was before me on the very same page of the total falsehood of the passage, when he knew that there was no such evidence there to be rejected. His *integrity* in that for the dear sake of gratifying feelings which I shall never envy, by flinging off the railing accusation of TOTAL FALSEHOOD OF STATEMENT, he has, ere he can take his breath, to recall his own fling and to shuffle from it with the pitiful qualification of predicating *total falsehood* of the statement, " *as it is professed to be understood,*" of which every logician knows that *total falsehood* is not predicable.

An illustration will exhibit this sophism in its true light:— Suppose one had said " King Charles the First was barbarously murdered," and had been answered, " It is a total falsehood of statement," by an opponent who instantly shrunk from this giving of the LIE-DIRECT into the COME-OFF,— "a total falsehood of statement as it is professed to be understood." What would be the inference but that *such* an answer had more the manners of a doctor of divinity, than of a gentleman, a greater prurience of abuse than pregnancy of argument?

I have not then made a false statement: I have not made a misquotation nor put forth a misrepresentation, no, nor the shadow of a misrepresentation; and he whom this good Christian politely calls "first born of calumny, and greatest liar that ever set pen to paper," is as far from being such as the sun's disc from darkness, or a Christian doctor's heart from charity.

As for the *error* (certainly not FALSEHOOD) which may or may not attach to any man's *understanding* of a particular statement, I hope I have as good a right to maintain my own understanding as I leave to all mankind the uncontrolled exercise of theirs: and could not have done so more fairly, more ingenuously and more honestly, than by putting forth *with* the statement which I *fairly quoted*, a reference to the work, volume, and page where it would be found; and that not by itself alone as *I* first found it,* but accompanied by the most powerful array of objection and controversy that the wit of man could possibly bring against it. I left these therefore to all the possible weight they could have on the mind, which my reference would direct to them: on *my own mind*, neither all their weight, with all that Dr. Smith can add to their weight, could overbalance the preponderance of the matter in its full effect to the intent for which I quoted it.

Reader, think'st thou, that one so ready to bring the

---

* In the works of Peter Annett, where it is given very incorrectly, but not falsely.

coarsest accusations in the coarsest language, would know what fairness, ingenuousness, and honesty were, when they stood before him in the enemy of his faith?

Now, reader, see and judge on what evidence this learned divine would bring the most frightful charge that could be alleged against any man, who was possessed of moral sensibility, and had some claim to be considered as good a scholar and as able a critic as himself.

What was the evidence before me in the very same page, of the total falsehood of the statement, as it is professed to be understood by some modern infidels? Why, the very next sentence after the statement itself, which I had fairly quoted, is Dr. Lardner's admission that "some have hence argued that the copies of the New Testament — of the Gospels at least — have not come down to us as they were originally written, they have been altered in the time of the emperor Anastasius, who began his reign in the year 491, and died in 518." Lardner, vol. 3, p. 67.

And why might not I enroll myself among those who argue thus, (and among whom are names of not inferior renown to any of their opponents,) sincerely believing as I do, that *they* have the best of the argument? Or why was it incumbent on me to have introduced into my Manifesto the objections of my adversaries — objections which I myself did not consider of sufficient validity to defeat or to alter the affect of my proposition? *

Or why should Dr. Lardner himself have introduced any notice at all of the existence of such a passage into this work, and have employed his great powers of augmentation, beating up for all the authorities, all the talent,

---

* Or why should Dr. Lardner's conflicting opinion be evidence to me, when in other cases, I had known and experienced the fallibility, not merely of his reasoning, but of his integrity?

learning and ingenuity he could find in the world, to come
"*to the help of the Lord — to the help of the Lord against
the mighty,*" if there were really no matter worth a consideration in this passage, or if there were sufficient evidence
of its total falsehood ? — which is so far from being the

Where the glory of God was concerned, and an ugly fact stood
bolt in the way of it, even Dr. Lardner would fight shy of letting us
know its true dimensions, and leave no stone unturned to contravene,
to conceal, suppress, or counteract its impressions on our convictions.
Victor Tununensis tells more than it is safe for Christian faith to
know. — Of course then, "*Victor is nobody,*" is the Christian argument, — and *Aye, but he has told it!* is mine; and it's well for him
that he is not to be found. Thus

AMMONIUS SACCUS,

The most distinguished ornament of the second century, had
taught that all the Gentile religions, and even the Christian, were to
be illustrated and explained by the principles of a universal philosophy, but that, in order to this, the fables of the priests were to be
removed from Paganism, and the comments and interpretations of
the disciples of Jesus from Christianity. Then Dr. Lardner could
not bring himself to admit that Ammonius was a Christian Father.
Fabricius had been equally illiberal, and indeed, I have found that
learned author still less to be trusted with the reputation of those
who differed from him, than Lardner. Mosheim had once been of
the same judgment, as to the character of Ammonius; but with
that greatness that always characterizes a master mind, he afterwards saw reason to change his opinion, and did so. His reasons
however, weigh little with Dr. Lardner, who opposes nothing to
them but mere assertion, unsupported by the smallest glimpse of
evidence. "The coalition between Platonism and Christianity, in
the second and third centuries, is a fact too fully proved, to be rendered dubious by mere affirmations." — Mosheim, vol. I. p. 170, the
Note.

Alas! the ravages of the religious pyrexia are but two discernible
upon the moral integrity, as well as on the physical capabilities,
even of great and good minds, what must be expected then from a
Rev. Dr. John Pye Smith, but such an answer as his is to the Manifesto of the Christian Evidence Society?

case that after making the best of all his apparatus in conflict against it, he conquers only in his own reckoning, the conclusion that

"*These considerations*, as *seem to me*, are sufficient to show that learned men have with good reason *generally* looked upon this story of Victor as fabulous." (p. 68.)

A conclusion which leaves the strength of my position unassailed. It is not evidence but *considerations* which have been brought against it — and considerations which, however sufficient they may seem to be to those who have the strongest possible interest in making the most of them, do not seem quite so sufficient to those who have considerations of which they have quite as good an opinion, and which have not yet been put into the scales.

Of course the advocates of Christianity will make the most and the best of all the evidence that will seem to serve their purpose; and will depreciate, disparage and decry the evidence that makes against them — aye! and disparage and decry it all the more, the more it makes against them. But with all their disparaging there is surely enough in the passage I have quoted and in the implied admissions of Dr. Lardner himself, to save the honor, honesty and truth of a man who might conscientiously differ from him, and might hold the passage to be genuine and valid, even his considerations against it, notwithstanding.

The *considerations* which Dr. Lardner quotes in his note from the Prolegomena of Dr. Mill to invalidate the passage, have much more effect in showing what a curse those Christian Scriptures have in all ages been to mankind, and what wicked dispositions they have ever engendered and have a direct tendency to engender, in men's bosoms, than to redeem their equivocal claim to genuineness and authenticity. "Indeed there is no saying what tragedies, what mighty tumults — not, perhaps, to have been allayed without the murder of the Emperor himself — the very name of new gospels would have excited throughout the whole East, &c., &c. Nor is there, that I know of, among the multitude of writers one, except Victor, and Isidore of Seville, who transcribed his words, who makes any mention of this *Radiurgy*." *

Has not this sword two edges? — and if we are to take into consideration that such was the temper and disposition of the Christian community, that they would have slain their Emperor and all the rest on't! had they but heard of an attempted alteration of their gospels, how can we shut out of our consideration its inseparable consequences, that truth and honesty had no fair chance; that one who had ventured to impeach the genuineness of those gospels though he had known, though he had witnessed the very act of forgery, would have been in danger of being torn in pieces; and every villanous and wicked art would be resorted to, to destroy his reputation and to suppress the discoveries he had made?

So that it is actually to the obscurity of the author, and to the circumstance of his writings not being commonly known, that we owe the happy event of their escaping the instant suppression to which, 'tis well known, that the Christians invariably assigned all the evidence that

---

* Ipsum nomen sane novorum evangeliorum, dici haud potest, quantas per universum Orientem, excitaturum fuisset tragœdias, quam graves tumultus nec fortasse sine Imperatoris cæde sopiendos.

. . . .

Neque extet quod sciam, ex omni scriptorum turbâ, præter unum Victorem, quique verba ejus transcripsit Isidoram Hispanensem qui ῥᾳδιεργίας hujus aliquam facit mentionem. — Mill. Proleg. p. 1015.

they found likely to make against them, to betray their secret or expose their folly.

Of this disposition to decry and to disparage their opponents, I shall not send the reader far to look for proofs.

Victor Tununensis, he sees, has betrayed the craft, he has left a sentence on record, that gravels the kidneys of orthodoxy. Very well, then Dr. John Pye Smith deprives him of his bishopric — and though it was on the very page before him that Victor Tununensis really was an African Bishop, Dr. John Pye Smith degrades him into "an obscure author, who wrote a Chronicle of about twelve pages," (though that happens to be twelve pages more than many Archbishops of Canterbury ever wrote,) and will never recognise him as a bishop, or apply to him any decent expression of courtesy or respect, any more than he would to the author of the Manifesto.

And after all the charges brought against the Manifesto, of total falsehood, of quoting books, chapters, pages, and passages, which say *no such thing* as is imputed to them; after the most rude and offensive forms of *flat denial*, that a spiteful heart could suggest and savage manners direct; the reader will see this good Christian admitting everything that I had maintained, endeavoring to make a poor excuse for *how it might come to be so*: and quoting his crony, Dr. Bentley, to bear off from himself the reproach of the gross and apparent *garbling*, which every eye must see, and every mind must be sensible of, in observing that the real words of the passage, "ab idiotis evangelistis composita," (composed by illiterate evangelists,) are turned into "ab idiotis librariis conscripta," (written by ignorant scribes,) which makes just exactly, all the difference.

As for the charge of total want of argumentative justice, let the reader look at *their* scale, and at *ours*: —

Quote *they* an Advocate for the Christian Argument? Why,

He shall be in a trice " the *Prince* of Critics," — " the glory of Scholars." Mr. Sharon Turner, and Mr. Hallam, the preachers, it may be in some canting Gospel-shop, shall have " dissipated the clouds that hung over the transactions of dark ages," &c.

But quote *we* an author who has *given tongue*, or let fall but a single sentence in their impediment? Why, like poor Judas Iscariot, he may go hang himself, and *his* bishopric shall another take.

Challenge they us to show, *when*, *where*, or *by whom* the Books of the New Testament could have been altered or corrected? We answer even to the exactitude of time, of place, of person. — They were so, WHEN Messela was consul, *i. e.* in the year 505, AT Constantinople, BY the command of the Emperor Anastasius — and they might have been so, at any time, or any where, or by any body.*

Challenge we them to show the infinitely more consequential points *when*, *where*, or *by whom* were the books of the New Testament, in the first instance, received, and

---

* Alexis Menesis Archbishop of Goa, ordered the Syriac Version of the N. T. to be altered according to the Latin Vulgate, and this command was executed with religious precision. At the end of the Syrian Manuscript of the four Gospels was the following subscription. " This sacred book was finished on Wednesday the eighteenth day of the first month Conun, (December) in the year 389 of the Greeks, *i. e.* in the year of Christ 78, by the hand of Achœus, a fellow laborer of Mar Maris, and a disciple of the Apostle Maradæus, whom we entreat to pray for us, Amen."— Marsh's Michælis, vol. 2., p. 28, 31.

recognised to be the compositions of the persons whose names they bear?

They can fix on *no* time, they can assign *no* place — they can give *no* name.

Mr. Sharon Turner, perhaps, Mr. Ebenezer Hallam, or our desperately flinging Doctor might make some discoveries; but all that Mosheim's Ecclesiastical History could communicate to one who happens to know no better Ecclesiastical History than that of Mosheim, is, that,

"The opinions or rather the conjectures of the learned concerning the time *when* the books of the New Testament were collected into one volume; as also about the *authors* of that collection, are extremely different, — this important question is attended with great and almost insuperable difficulties to us in these later times." Mosheim, vol. 1., part 2., chap. 2., sect. 16., page 108., edit. 8vo., London 1811. — "Not long after Christ's ascension into heaven, several histories of his life and doctrine, full of pious frauds, and fabulous wonders, were composed by persons whose intentions, perhaps, were not bad, but whose writings discovered the greatest superstition and ignorance. Nor was this all; productions appeared which were imposed upon the world by fraudulent men, as the writings of the holy apostles." Ibid. p. 109.

Now the reader has only to compare this statement, supported as it is, by internal evidence, Luke v. 1. (Forasmuch as many have taken in hand to set forth in order, &c.,) with Dr. Lardner's Table of the times and places, when and where he *conjectures* that the several Books of the New Testament *might have been* written: and he will see, to a demonstration, that the "histories of Christ's life and doctrines, full of pious frauds and fabulous wonders, that were written not long after his ascension," had the precedency of all the writings now contained in the NEW TESTAMENT: and that, therefore, those "pious frauds and fabulous wonders" were not depravations and corruptions of the Gospel narratives: but the Gospel narratives are only castigated and improved editions of those original "pious frauds and fabulous wonders." Nor was it only on vulgar and uncultivated minds that these "pious frauds and fabulous wonders," could have been originally imposed, or have long retained their credit;— *that* part of every man's mind which is surrendered to the influence of religion, is always vulgar and uncultivated. Our all-accomplished ADDISON, the author of the Spectator, even the *Protestant* Addison, had the bleak heath or common in his mind, extensive enough to give growth to a firm faith in one of the grossest of those pious frauds. In his Evidences of the Truth of the Christian religion, he adduces his own belief of the genuineness and authenticity of the Letter which Jesus Christ wrote to Abgarus, King of Edessa; if we believe Nicephorus, ἰδίαις χερσί * with his own hands. As for the arguments

---

* Of this Letter of Christ, and of the Letter of Abgarus, which opened the correspondence, Fabricius says, "Has Epistolas ita ut ab Eusebio prolatæ sunt, in Archivis extitisse Edessenis, non puto esse dubitandum. Neque quicquam in illis continetur indignum Christo, neque si pro genuinis habeantur error aliquis ex illis confirmari poterit." Codex Apocryphus N. T. Johanne Alberto Fabricio, Hamburgi, Anno 1703. Tom. i. p. 319.— The folly of Addison is further kept in countenance by the sympathy of Divines of high renown in the Protestant Church, Montacute, Parker, Cave, and Grape, though sufficiently scouted by the (in this respect) less credulous doctors of the Romish Community. Ibid. 320. The religious affection, like every other species of insanity, has its lucid intervals. But though the belief of improbabilities, on the report of others, is clearly to be ascribed to weakness of understanding, *quoad hoc;*

which Dr. Smith puts forth in such HIGH-HORSE sort of style, as if to carry the convictions of his hearers by storm; that any alteration of the text of the Gospels was impracticable, impossible, intolerable — not to have been attempted, or not to have been endured. An' I were sure he would open upon me a fresh volley of that kind of language which I can never return, and call me the *first-born of calumny*, and swear that there was *no such a passage*, and that it was *a gross forgery*, I'd venture to whisper to some of his hearers, that " it is a certain fact, that several readings, in our common printed text, are nothing more than *alterations* made by Origen, whose authority was so great in the Christian church, that *emendations* which he proposed, though, as he himself acknowledged, they were supported by the evidence of *no manuscript*, were very generally received;" and the Lord Bishop of Peterboro', in whose diocese I am now a prisoner, and of whose Divinity Lectures, in the University of Cambridge, I was once a pupil — told me as much — and, reader, would'st thou turn to Michælis's Introduction to the New Testament, translated by Bishop Marsh, vol.

---

yet this excuse cannot extend to those who propose improbabilities to the faith of others — and scepticism itself would not suppose that Saint Augustin could, with any propriety, be suspected of being a FOOL, when in his 33d Sermon, addressed to his reverend brethren, he says, " I was already Bishop of Hippo, when I went into Ethiopia with some servants of Christ, there to preach the Gospel. In this country we saw many men and women without heads, who had two great eyes in their breasts; and in countries still more southerly, we saw a people who had but one eye in their foreheads."

This is as true as the Gospel. This same Holy Father bears an unequally unquestionable testimony to several resurrections of the

2., part 1, edit. 3, Lond., 1819, chap. 9, page 368, he should tell thee no less.

And could'st thou read Latin, or give me credit for quoting a bit from my memory which, in *this house of bondage*, I am obliged to make my best bargain of—though I cannot give the chapter, page, and verse, thou should'st hold me worthy of so much reliance as to let me persuade thee that FELE, Bishop of Oxford, has somewhere said,

"Tanta fuit primis seculis fingendi licentia, tam prona in credendo facilitas ut rerum gestarum fides exinde graviter labōraverit. Neque enim orbis terrarum tantum, sed et Dei Ecclesia de temporibus suis mysticis merito queratur;" and not having the advantage of finding it ready translated, as I did the passage from VICTOR — I supply thee with my guess at it — "Such was the license of inventing, so headlong the readiness of believing in the first ages — that the credibility of transactions derived from thence must have been hugely doubtful — nor has the world only, but the Church of God also, has reasonably to complain of its mystical times,"— and SCALIGER, a scholar and a critic well learned in these researches, though not "the Glory of Scholars," nor "the Prince of Critics," somewhere says, "Omnia quæ putabant Christianismo conducere — bibliis suis interseruerunt" — which I, not having learned all the languages that may be taught at Homerton College — take to mean little more or less than that "they put into their Bibles any thing that they thought would serve the craft," *i. e.*, that they thought would conduce to Christianity; and when they thought that

---

dead, of which he himself had been an eye-witness. See Middleton's Free Inquiry, *in loco*. Of all travellers in the world, Christian Missionaries are the most famous for seeing strange things.

any particular scripture would not serve the craft, it was not the name nor the authority of an Apostle that would save either *it* or *him* from being rejected. But reader! take the Rev. Dr. Smith's word for it! that this is " a shameless lie, an impudent falsehood, and that there is no authority whatever for asserting or inferring any such thing;" and do it DEVOUTLY! and say thy *prayers* over it! and when thou hast well nigh prayed thine eyes out, thou wilt see nothing of the kind to be inferred from the 9th and 10th verses of the only chapter of the Third Epistle of St. John; though thou hast before thee " confirmation strong as proof of holy writ;" and thou wilt leave it only to such a miserable man as the Manifesto writer to sympathize in the wrongs of a rejected Apostle, and to say Poor Johnny, Poor favorite of Christ! So they turned thee and thy writings out of the church! and who the Devil wrote the rigmarole that the rogues have passed off as the Gospel according to Saint John, all the while?

Sufficient presumption, however, of the power of other Emperors as well as Anastasius, to foist whatever scriptures they pleased on the easy faith of Christians, will be found in still existing proofs of the fact of their suppressing the evidence that might have exposed the villany of the whole system. I here present the reader with the substance of a formal decree of the evangelical Emperor Theodosius, to this purport.

THE DECREE.

"We decree, therefore, that all writings, whatever which Porphyry, or any one else hath written against the Christian Religion in the possession of whomsoever they shall be found should be committed to the fire; for we would not suffer any of those things so much as to come to men's ears, which tend to provoke God to wrath and to offend the minds of the pious." *

A similar decree of this Emperor for establishing the doctrine of the Trinity, concludes with an admonition to all who shall object to it, that "Besides the condemnation of divine justice they must expect to suffer the severe penalties which our authority, guided by heavenly wisdom, may think proper to inflict upon them."—Quoted by Gibbon, vol. 5, p. 15.

SECTION IV.

ON THE ASSERTION THAT ARCHBISHOP LANFRANC EFFECTED AN ALTERATION OF THE SCRIPTURES.

THE section thus headed in the Answer to the Manifesto, would almost induce a guess that our angry doctor had learned his logic of St. Patrick; it sheathes the vinegar of intended accusation in the oil of palpable absurdity. To prove, you see, that there was no such thing as an account of a general alteration of the Scriptures to accommodate them to the faith of the orthodox, in the passage which I had referred to as containing such an account:—he finds the passage agreeably to the reference I had given him, he produces it in his own note,

---

* Sancimus igitur ut omnia quæcumque Porphyrius aut quivis alius contra religiosum Christianorum cultum, conscripsit, apud quemcumque inventa fuerint, igni mancipentur, omnia enim provocantia Deum ad iracundiam scripta, et pias mentes offendentia, ne ad aures quidem hominum venire volumus."—Quoted by Lardner vol. 4., p. 111.

and there to be sure the account is and as I quoted it in full effect, and to all the intent and purpose for which I quoted it, answering like the impressed wax to the engraven seal. O wicked forger, as in his account I still should be, though I were as the God of truth himself, without variableness or shadow of turning.

To perceive the absurdity of the accusations in this sentence, let the reader but run them over with the most obvious questions to himself that a moment's pause upon them must suggest.

1. "The passage in Beausobre contains no such thing." &c. *Answer.* And there the thing *is* subjoined in a note by the denier of the thing himself.

2. "And its evident meaning is," &c. *Answer.* Paddy is going to give us the evident meaning of that of which he has just told us, "*there is no such thing.*"

3. "Lanfranc directs a revisal and correction to be made of certain copies that were in his possession, or to which his agents could have access." *Answer.* DOES HE so? And who ever accused him of directing a revisal and correction to be made of copies that were *not* in his possession, or to which his agents could *not* have access?

4. "There are several questions connected with this statement, which ought to be fairly investigated, before we can form any decided opinion in the case." *Answer.* Not if there were no such thing as the statement itself: and if there *were* such a statement, should not the several questions have been investigated first, and the decided opinion suspended?

5. "Lanfranc, a man of good personal character, rivetting the chains of ecclesiastical slavery." *Answer.* What is a good personal character? or would it not have been better for mankind, if he had not been quite so good, and

so had not rivetted the chains quite so fast, — what is it to you, or me, reader, if those who chain us to the earth, keep fast on Friday?

6. "The documents of history, &c., are very obscure." *Answer.* So, so!!

7. "Those errors have been dissipated only very lately, by Mr. Sharon Turner, Mr. Hallam, and other eminent men of the present day." *Answer.* Saving their eminences' dignity, I warrant ye, they are no better than Methodist parsons, and owe all their eminence to their conformity to the opinions of Dr. John Pye Smith, or to the exhibition of their "human faces divine," in the Evangelical Magazine.

8. "Every printer and bookseller perfectly well knows, and many readers of books know to their vexation, that even in the present day, when the art of printing renders accuracy so much more easy to be attained, many editions of good books are sent out shamefully incorrect." *Answer.* Is not this EVERY THING? and does it leave the possibility of either candor or piety, or of having any *rational* fear of God before his eyes, to the man who will dare to maintain that a God of mercy, truth, and power, would or could have given to man, a written, or book-contained revelation? *

---

* *A written, or book-contained revelation.* "God is just, equal and, good, and as sure as he is so, so he cannot put the salvation and happiness of any man, upon what he has not put it in the power of any man on earth to be entirely satisfied of." — Bishop of Salisbury's Preservative, p 78, as quoted by Tindal, 414.

Bishop Jeremy Taylor, in his polemical works, page 521, after enumerating the vast variety of causes of difficulty and misunderstanding in revelation, concludes thus, "These, and a thousand more, have made it more impossible for any man in so great a variety of matter, not to be deceived." "There is scarce any church

9. "Had Lanfranc's party made alterations of the smallest importance, it is morally impossible but the facts would have been placed in a clear light, and the evidence of them would have come down to posterity." *Answer,* by Dr. Smith himself, " The documents of history for that period, and some centuries after, are very obscure."

10. "It is worthy of observation, that Lanfranc is remarked by Dr. Cave (Historia Literaria, vol. 2, p. 148,) to have been addicted to the making of alterations in the text, which he conceived to be amendments."

Answer. It is indeed worthy of observation, and I hope the reader will observe it, and ask himself if his imagination could conceive a droller way than this of refuting the statement made in the Manifesto. The doctor's reckoning of refutation to the Manifesto, then, as the sum of this section, stands thus —

1st. There is no such thing as an account of a general alteration of the Scriptures to accommodate them to the faith of the orthodox; because, *there* the account actually is, quoted by the doctor himself from the very work in which it was stated that the account was.

2d. It is morally impossible, that such an alteration could have taken place, without more ample evidence of it coming down to posterity: because, every thing that was done in those dark ages, was sure to be set in the clearest light.

---

in Christendom at this day which does not obtrude, not only plain falsehoods, but such falsehood as will appear to any free spirit, pure contradictions and impossibilities, and that, with the same gravity, authority, and importunity, as they do the holy oracles of God."— Dr. Henry More, Mystery of Godliness, 495, quoted in Tindal, 314.

Take heed and beware, lest any man deceive you; believe them not!— *Ascribed to Jesus Christ.*— Because that which may be known of God is manifest.— Romans i., 19.

3d. It was morally impossible that Archbishop Lanfranc could have altered the Scriptures : because he was peculiarly addicted to the making of alterations in the text, which he conceived to be amendments : and,

4th. Even supposing that Archbishop Lanfranc had procured the alteration of the Gospels, to accommodate them to the orthodox faith in England, when England was rivetted in the chains of ecclesiastical slavery, and bowed to a servility of subjection to the Pope, yet we are to infer how impossible it was that any like or other alterations could have been made in the Gospels of France, Spain, and Italy, which, you see, were so much further removed from papal influence.

11. "I now appeal," says the liberal D. D., "to any man of sense, whether it is not most unfair and absurd, to represent this obscure and dubious circumstance, and which is at most of no real importance, as in the smallest degree impugning the Scriptures."

To which I answer, that I also appeal to any man of sense, whether it was not quite as unfair in Dr. Smith, to set out with denying *in toto*, the existence of an account, which he at last admits and endeavors to explain away, to have impeached an author's veracity without material to fortify his impeachment, and to have given such hard names, as the prelude to such soft arguments.

Κυνος ομματ' εχων, κραδιην δ'ελαφοιο.

SECTION V.

ON THE NATURE OF VARIOUS READINGS, AND THE INFERENCES TO BE DRAWN FROM THEM.

1. " The pretended reference to the Unitarian New Version, is another instance of most disgraceful ignorance, or shameless perversion. " So says the Rev. Dr. John Pye Smith, and one is the more sorry that he should say so; because it spoils the heading of the best written section in his book, in which the reader might otherwise be as pleased as I am to bear witness to Dr. John Pye Smith's able writing, deep learning, and ingenious reasoning. — There was all the less occasion to have introduced so clever a performance with so paltry a prologue. — The reader however, will, I hope, do my adversary the justice, to brush off this unworthiness, and let the subsequent matter stand in undiminished claim on the respect it merits. All that concerns the Manifesto or its author in this section (which is all that is amiss in it,) — will be answered in the reader's observance — that the pretended reference to the Unitarian New Version, cannot at any rate be *another* instance of ignorance or perversion, — unless some *one* instance of ignorance or perversion had preceded it — which is *not* the case.

Neither can the reference with any propriety be called " *pretended*," if it be a *real* one — if the passage affecting to be quoted is there exactly to be found in the book and page from which it purports to be made — which *is* the case.

And of which, to remove all doubt, the doctor cites " the passage fairly and fully," in which — by his own showing is all and every thing that I *did* quote, and to the full effect and intent for which I quoted it; and much further matter to the same effect,— a droll way this of convicting a man of "*falsely pretending to quote.*"

But as "*falsely pretending to quote,*"— were rather strong words,— and in the general meaning and acceptation of them would stand but awkwardly applied to immediate evidence of the most accurate and literal quotation that could possibly be made; the doctor himself softens off the more revolting point of the charge by subjoining the wholly incompatible and contradictory meaning of his own, "*the tendency and application of which he has grossly perverted.*"

Upon the tendency and application of a passage,— I hope *one* man has as good a right to exercise his own judgment as *another;* but sure a man's "perverting the *tendency* and *application* of a passage," is a charge which in itself involves his acquittal from the charge of falsely pretending to quote it.

2. To the doctor's charge of the alternative of ignorance or dishonesty of which he bids his "worthy countrymen" judge against me, (p. 22.) I put in his own discharge from the former (page 60.) "*It is not ignorance;*" and to the latter I put in both the title and contents of this section itself:

The title admitting — that there are "VARIOUS READINGS," and therefore I have not represented a thing — which was not:

The contents admitting — that " the number of various readings collected by Dr. Mill is computed at thirty thousand, and that a hundred thousand at least have been *added* to the *list.* Therefore, so surely as thirty thousand with a hundred thousand added thereto — doth amount to

ONE HUNDRED AND THIRTY THOUSAND, — which is the thing and is what I have represented, I have not misrepresented the thing which is.

If there be arithmetic in this — there is no room for the charge of dishonesty, and Dr. Smith's anger has outrun his wit.

3. But the superscription of this section will serve us — further than this in its important clause — "AND OF THE INFERENCES THAT ARE TO BE DRAWN."

Reader, if thou art a true and genuine Protestant thou wilt draw what inference thou pleasest, and maintain — not only thy right — but thy *ability* to draw an inference for thyself as well as any man can draw it for thee; and to be unattainted either of dishonesty or of ignorance, though thy inferences should be the diametrical reverse of the inferences which Dr. John Pye Smith, or his holiness the Pope,— who never arrogated more than this Dr. John Pye Smith, would draw for thee.

If thou art a staunch Papist or (what is not in principle a whit less papistical,) a priest-worshipping dissenter,— why Dr. Smith's inferences will of course be infallible with thee — and well may be so.

But as for the legitimate and uncontroled drawing of inferences, it becomes a writer who would *assist* and not coerce the reason of his reader, to submit his views as inferences which *may be* drawn, not as inferences which *must*, or as the only inferences which ARE TO BE DRAWN, not in impediment of the equal right of another to draw the most opposite inferences, — but in recognition and deference to that right.

The main tact, however, equally incumbent on the observance of all reasoners is, that their inferences in any extent of their divergency — keep still their hold upon the original *nucleus* fact itself, and by no means of chicane and sophistry, be slipt on to some counterfeit or mistake of the fact, which must render the best spun reasoning in the world inconsequential.

Thus, it is in logic an *Ignoratio Elenchi,* an entire substitution of a matter that was *not* in question for the matter that *was :* when the combination of chances which is sufficient to go to sleep on as a good *guess,* — for what *might have been* the original text of Homer, Herodotus or Hippocrates; (it being of no consequence what that text was,) is to be held sufficient to assure us of the sense of a divine revelation, in which to be wrong — may lead to our taking that which was forbidden for that which was commanded; and in which to suppose the alternative indifferent is to withdraw the matter at issue.

4. Be it that out of the hundred and thirty thousand various readings which the doctor, after having charged me with the grossest falsehood for having put forth such an assertion, himself asserts, — " those which produce any material difference in the sense, are extremely few indeed." (See his note, p. 56.)

Yet, " *extremely few indeed,*" must in any arithmetic, be more than a couple out of a hundred and thirty thousand : not to say that on the *preliminary* and infinitely important question as to what constitutes a *material difference,* we have to rely on the judgment of those who have the strongest possible interest in causing the difference to appear as immaterial as possible.

Thus it is well known that in one of the early editions of the English Bible, the seventh commandment stood thus, — THOU SHALT COMMIT ADULTERY; and many thousands of good Christians understood and obeyed God's holy commandment, according to this the commonly received reading. A various reading has since introduced the important particle,—NOT, so that the amended text became diametrically reversed and stood, "THOU SHALT NOT COMMIT ADULTERY." The advocates and observers of the commandment, however, according to its *original* acceptation, would no doubt contend for *their* reading of it, or at least that the difference was *immaterial*.

And there is good reason to think and high authority to *infer*, that the letter of the sixth commandment must originally have been in a similar predicament and have stood—THOU SHALT DO MURDER; not merely because Saint Paul expressly says—"*the letter killeth;*"—(which to be sure he means of the letter of the *New Testament,*) yet the history of the *People of God*, is little short of a demonstration—that they never could have understood that murder was a thing which God had forbidden.

The introduction of the negative particle NO, in this passage, not only sets it at variance with the known mind and will of the God of Israel,—by whom the most sanguinary murders, and butcheries of "women and children, infants and sucklings," were expressly commanded; but is unsupported, by any authority, or countenance of any other part of those "*lively oracles*"—there not being another passage to be found in the whole Bible, wherein,—where murder, cruelty and butchery of any sort is spoken of, that God says NO to it. And if this reading of the passage—*without* the negative or inhibitory particle be objected to, on account of the manifest absurdity of supposing a positive command to commit murder: we answer, what would become of one half of God's word, if manifest absurdity were any valid ground of objection against it? Restore, then, the primitive purity of God's word: let the texts stand, THOU SHALT COMMIT ADUL-

TERY! THOU SHALT MURDER! THOU SHALT STEAL! and THOU SHALT BEAR FALSE WITNESS! the practice of both Jews and Christians will be found to quadrate with this sense of their rule of duty, and to all the objections of sceptics, and the scoffings of infidels — we answer in the language of the *Prince of Critics*, (p. 25.) "What a scheme would these men make? What worthy rules would they prescribe to providence, (p. 26.,) and pray to what great use or design? To give satisfaction to a few obstinate and untractable wretches; to those who are not convinced by Moses and the prophets, but want one from the dead to 'come and convert them!'" (p. 27.)

See, reader! how unavoidably one falls into the language of keenest sarcasm, when one only attempts — I say not, (for I am not Prince of Critics, that I should assume the prerogative of saying,) to "*answer a fool according to his folly,*" (p. 26,) but to answer a Doctor of Divinity, in the parity of his own reasons, and the application of his own language.

But, reader, contemplate the facts, — not as stated by me, an avowed unbeliever, and martyr to the just and glorious cause of unbelief — but my good service, wrung, and wrenched out from the conquered concessions, and unwilling admissions of those who would never have made thee so wise, but for our conquest.

FACTS ADMITTED.	INFERENCES.
5. "The possessors of these costly treasures had not the means, nor, perhaps, were expert in the method of comparing two or more copies together, in order to ascertain the correctness of each. (p. 20.)	5. "It was much easier to introduce interpolations when copies were few and scarce, than since they have been multiplied by means of the press. Unit. Version of the N. T. (p. 121.)
6. "Variations from the original copy, purely accidental, but sometimes from design. (p. 20.)	6. "How often — was, *sometimes*, and to what aim and gist did the *designed variations* extend?
7. "The ART of determining the true reading, out of several variations most important. (p. 20.)	7. "Who is master of that art? and on what principle can others rely on his ability?
8. "Quotations may be, in some respects, superior to manuscripts. (p. 21.)	8. "What respect could those who thought so, have paid to the pretended originals?
9. "Very few of the various readings produce any alteration in the meaning of a sentence still less *(fewer)* in the purport of a whole paragraph. (p. 21.) NOTE! — But sometimes the whole paragraph itself, was altogether a forgery; as, for instance, Acts ix. 5, 6, which Erasmus himself foisted in without authority of any manuscript whatever. — See Marsh, vol. 2, p. 496.	9. "How *many* are very few? and who is to judge of the effect of the alteration upon the original meaning? It is admitted that alterations of the inspired word of God have been made to the full extent of altering the purport of whole paragraphs — whose word then doth it become, having been so altered? — Produce a title deed to a forty shilling freehold, before a Court of Justice, in *such* a predicament, and what would be said to your pretensions?

10. "The consequence is, that of no ancient books whatsoever, do we possess a text so critically correct, so satisfactorily perfect, as that which exists in the best editions of the Hebrew and Greek Scriptures. (p. 22.) This consequence, is itself only an inference — but — *Valeat!*

10. "*The most critically correct;* but who, being the critics? *The most satisfactorily perfect;* but who being satisfied? *The best editions* — but which being the best editions? And what approach, shall being the correctest, the perfectest, and the best type of an ancient book be, to its being the WORD OF GOD, which he who believeth not, shall be damned? The snail that out-gallops all other snails, is yet no race-horse.*

FACTS ADMITTED IN THE UNITARIAN VERSION..

INFERENCES WHICH MAY BE DRAWN.

1. "In those variations which in some measure affect the sense, the true reading often shines forth with a lustre of evidence, which is perfectly satisfactory to the judicious inquirer. — (23.)

1. "*In some measure affect the sense* — is it of no consequence in what measure? *The true reading* — which is that? — *Perfectly satisfactory to the judicious inquirer;* that is to say — and if it is not satisfactory to you, you are a fool, or as the PRINCE OF CRITICS would call you, an obstinate untractable wretch.*

2. "The various readings which affect the doctrines of Christianity are very few. — (24.)

2. "Two? six? ten? fifty? a hundred? or only, perhaps, so few as two or three thousand?*

FACTS ADMITTED IN THE UNITARIAN VERSION.	INFERENCES WHICH MAY BE DRAWN.
3. " Yet some of these are of great importance.	3. " Very orthodox this! Some of the various readings which *do* affect the doctrines of Christianity, it seems are not of great importance.
4. " Of those passages which can be justly regarded as wilful interpolations, the number is very small indeed.	4. " *Very small, indeed :* only, perhaps, half a bushel. — *Wilful Interpolations !* Does any iota of the Manifesto now want proof or demonstration ?
5. " 1 John v. 7, is by far the most notorious, and most universally acknowledged and reprobated. NOTE ! — " In our common editions of the Greek Testament, are MANY readings, which exist not in a single manuscript, but are founded on MERE CONJECTURE." — Marsh, vol. 2, p. 496.	5. " Most notorious ! Good God ! and some are skulking yet, undetected, and so not quite so notorious ? Yet is the whole circulated as of equal authority ; the whole, and as it is known to be false, and acknowledged to be forged, read in our churches, and invariably spoken of as the faithful and unerring Word of God ——— God, for thy Mercy ! But they do it DEVOUTLY !

FACTS ADMITTED IN THE UNITARIAN VERSION, BUT NOT REFERRED TO BY DR. SMITH.	INFERENCES WHICH MAY BE DRAWN.
6. " It is notorious, that the orthodox charge the heretics with corrupting the	6. " They do, indeed, and when the orthodox have corrupted one half, and the

FACTS ADMITTED IN THE UNITARIAN VERSION, BUT NOT REFERRED TO BY DR. SMITH.	INFERENCES WHICH MAY BE DRAWN.
text, and that the heretics recriminate upon the orthodox. — (p. 121.)	heretics have corrupted the other, all the rest on't may be depended on as genuine.
7. "It is notorious that forged writings, under the names of the Apostles, were in circulation almost from the Apostolic age." — See 2 Thess. ii. 2.	7. "The tracing of a writing up to the Apostolic age, would, therefore, afford no presumption of its genuineness: the name of an Apostle is no proof that the writing is not the composition of an impostor."

The reader may receive or reject these inferences or supply any other, or contrary inferences, of his own; and shall assuredly be safe from any imprecations, denunciations, or prayers of mine: "those let them employ, who need, or when they need, not I!" All that I require is, his observance of the facts themselves; and that to these facts may now be added the fact, that the Rev. Dr. John Pye Smith has impeached the veracity of the Manifesto Writer, without adducing an iota of evidence to support his impeachment — a fact upon which it is as unnessary as it would be unbecoming of me to suggest an inference. Doctor John Pye Smith is a preacher of the Everlasting Gospel; and when he impeaches the veracity of others, has, no doubt, higher ends in view, than to admit of his attending to the accuracies of language himself. *The truth of God* so entirely fills the mind of an evangelical preacher, that he has no room to pay any regard to truth, in his dealings with the sons of men. In their controversies with unbelievers, the saints have not only acted upon the principle of stopping at nothing, but avowed and justified it, even because " those who reject the truth as it is in Jesus," as they say, forfeit all right to have any sort of truth, either told to them, or spoken of them.

SECTION VI.

ON THE STORY OF THE ROCKET MAKER.

The manuscripts from which the received text was taken, were stolen by the librarian, and sold to a sky-rocket maker, in the year 1749.

1. " If we had not already seen such disgusting instances of the falsehood and audacity of this Manifesto Writer, one could scarcely have thought it possible that any man would make and publish such base misrepresentations, and hold them forth too, as quotations from eminent authors." — (p. 27.)

This language is really frightful, and were not its barb broken off, by the accompanying qualifications of the, *had we not already* " SEEN SUCH DISGUSTING INSTANCES," &c., where, certainly, no such instance had been seen at all, 'twould take a stouter heart than mine, to bear up against it. But by this time, the reader must have perceived, that Dr. Smith is more terrible in accusation, than formidable in proof. He charges in thunder; he hits in smoke; a puff of wind dissipates his caliginous armament, and leaves all the strong lines of our impregnable fortress unshaken and unmoved. Indeed it may stand as one of the happiest exemplifications of the native genius of priestcraft, and the best resulting *moral* of this controversy to observe that in exact proportion as his arguments grow weaker and weaker, his passions become more violent; his language more intemperate; his accusations more temerarious; his malice — more : —

No! *no more malice; that* vessel was running over from the first. So far from the story of the rocket-maker as glanced at in the Manifesto being an instance of falsehood or audacity; or falsely represented as resting on the authority of eminent authors; it is an instance of the most heedful fidelity and punctilious accuracy. The reader has only, once for all, to observe what the plan of the Manifesto is, and how much matter was to be compressed into how small a compass; and he will see that no full or extensive account of any matter was there intended, or indeed, possible; but an index only of the fact itself was given with a reference to the work, volume, and page, where the full and extensive account of it *would be* found.

And so heedfully faithful was the Author of the Manifesto, that even the so many words as indicated the fact, were not without their authority : but taken from the *eminent* authors of the Unitarian Version, in their Introduction, Sect. 3, entitled *Brief account of the received text,* &c. where the reader will see, (page 8. line 1,) the words — " The manuscripts from which it was published, are now irrecoverably lost, having been sold by the librarian, to a rocket maker, about the year 1750." And so punctiliously accurate was the Author of the Manifesto, that, not content even with the authority of the Editors of the Unitarian Version, when they spoke so loosely as to say merely that the "librarian sold the manuscripts," without saying by what right;* and "to a rocket-maker," without saying what sort of rockets; and "about the year 1750," without naming the year exactly. The Author of the Manifesto indagated the high source from which the Unitarian Editors themselves had derived *their* information; and from *that* indisputable fountain of learning and authority, giving the most accurate reference to work, volume and page, he supplied the more precise statement by which the reader understands that the librarian was a *thief;* that the rockets were *sky*-rockets; and that it was in the year 1749. Nay, I have been more punctilious than Dr. Smith had the means of being; for whereas he on the authority of this great critic, decries the Complutensian Polyglot which is the basis of the received text, and endeavors to show that the manuscripts from which it was formed were *few*, of no great antiquity and of *little value;* in order to make it appear that they might be very well spared and that it was of no consequence; yet for all this (strongly as it savors of the sour-grape reasoning) *he* has only the authority of the Bishop of Peterborough, as far as it will serve him in the edition from which *he* quotes, which is the edition of 1793, whereas in the later edition which is that from which *I* quote, (the edition of 1819,) he will find that the good Bishop has *changed his mind* on this subject and set him an example, which best becomes a wise and good man, safe enough from the imitation of a *Dissenterian* Theologue, an example of willingness to acknowledge the force of superior reasoning.

"Though I was of a different opinion," says the candid

---

* By what right? — STOLEN, says the Manifesto. — So *villanously purloined*, (p. 30,) says the Answerer of the Manifesto.

bishop, "*when I published the second edition* of this introduction, I am thoroughly persuaded *at present* that Goeze is in the right; nor do I consider it as a disgrace to acknowledge an error into which I had fallen for want of having seen the edition itself. With respect to Wetstein, though he is a declared enemy of this edition, yet what has frequently excited my astonishment, the readings which he has preferred to the COMMON text are, in most cases found in the Complutensian Greek Testament. He degrades it, therefore, in words but honors it in fact." Michælis's Introduction to the New Testament, translated by Bishop Marsh, vol. 2, part 1, chap. xii., sect. 1., page 439, line 33, THE THIRD EDITION. London, 1819.

2. "Now I appeal to the ingenuous reader," says Dr. Smith, "and ask how dishonorable, base, and wicked must be that man's soul, &c., who can, from this transaction, tell the public that the manuscripts from which the received texts of the New Testament were taken were thus made away with. If he really believed what he wrote, how miserably incompetent — and how dishonest!"

AVAST! AVAST! Here is more railing than any man who had truth on his side, or who but *thought* he had, would have had any occasion for.

The reader will only be pleased to observe, that Dr. Smith gives no definition of what the received text is, and therefore reserves his opportunity of evasion from a complete demonstration of the truth of the Manifesto, by his coarse and abusive flat denials of the most palpable and apparent evidence: but as 'tis with the reader only that I have to deal, I beg leave to refer him to the Introduction to the Unitarian New Version, where he will find *fully* set forth the facts, which I thus abridge.

1. The received text of the New Testament is that which is in general use. — Sect. 3, vii.

2. In the beginning of the sixteenth century, Cardinal Ximenes printed, at Alcala, in Spain, a copy of the New Testament in Greek, which was made from a collation of various manuscripts which were then thought to be of great authority, but which are now known to be of little value ; * this edition is called the Complutensian Polyglot. They were the manuscripts from which this Complutensian Polyglot was formed, that were thus disposed of.

3. But is was this Complutensian Polyglot (which was not licensed for publication till A. D. 1522, though it had been printed many years before) of which Robert Stephens availed himself for the formation of his splendid edition, published A. D. 1550.

4. And it was this edition of Robert Stephens's, which became the basis of the Elzevir edition, published at Leyden, A. D. 1624.

5. And this Elzeyir edition constitutes the received text. Therefore, if the reader hath but logic enough to connect the first and last link of a Sorites, so as to perceive, that whatever was the basis of A, after B had

---

* But the reader must observe, that the editors of the Unitarian Version, published in 1808, had not the advantage of Bishop Marsh's *later* and *more correct* opinion, and of the excellent reasons which he gives for that later and more correct opinion, in his edition of 1819, or they would, in all probability, have altered their own judgment of an edition which now holds to itself the high character of a Codex Criticus. He will observe, too, with what complacent philosophy even Unitarian Divines play Fox with us, and take upon themselves to give us their word for it, that the manuscripts, which 'tis certain they know nothing about, "are now known to have been of but little value."

been built upon A, and C had been built upon B, would have been the basis of C also; he must see that the manuscripts from which the Complutensian Polyglot was taken, are the manuscripts from which the received text was taken. And it being undeniably true, that the manuscripts from which the Complutensian Polyglot was taken, were sold by the librarian, who had no right to sell them, (to *Toryo*, the rocket-maker,) the truth of the terms of the Manifesto are involved in that truth. And it is *incontrovertibly true*, that the manuscripts from which the received text was taken, were stolen by the librarian, and sold to a sky-rocket maker in the year 1749,* as stated in the Manifesto.

---

* The Unitarian editors seem not to have a much better opinion of the received text, than those who have the worst, since *they* say of it:—" From the few advantages which were possessed, and from the little care which was taken by the early editors, it may be justly concluded, not only that the received text is *not* a perfect copy of the apostolic originals, but that," (*Unitar. New Version, Introd. London Edit.* 1808, *section* 3, *page* 9, *line* 39 *from the top*, 4 *from the bottom.*) Let them say on! and let Dr. John Pye Smith say that they say no such thing as is imputed to them, but indeed the very contrary, that it is an impudent forgery, and an unblushing falsehood. The reader has, by this time, learned how Dr. Smith's accusations are to be estimated! and his own morals will have received no ill lesson from the demonstration that his treatise supplies, that the greatest disposition to give the lie, is generally the concomitant of the least ability to prove it. It is due, however, to historical fidelity, to state, that there are much better editions than that of the received text, supplied and enriched by manuscripts that were not in the possession of the Complutensian editors. And that Toryo, the rocket-maker, of course destroyed those manuscripts of both Testaments only, which had been used for *that* edition. But *that* edition being the basis of the received text, the fact could not, in an Index, which is all that the Manifesto purports to be, have been more accurately stated. — It is truth itself.

The alternative of dishonor, baseness, and wickedness, if it could not have been suspended by charity, and by that reluctance which good men generally feel to draw so harsh a conclusion, is superseded now, by the verdict of evidence itself. — NOT GUILTY!

For the alternative of *miserable incompetence*, I leave the scales of decision between the doctor's literary pretensions and mine entirely in the hand of the reader, not caring on which side the preponderance may be, nor feeling any apprehension or envy of the *unapparent* and *unknown* learning which the doctor may in the back-ground really possess; but weighing what appears and judging by what can be judged, the reader will observe that the temple of Minerva has been as open to the Manifesto Writer as to the Doctor of Divinity, and that where the Doctor quotes an eminent author, the Manifests Writer quotes that same author after he had become *more eminent* than when the doctor knew him: and had revised and corrected those opinions for the better and more competent information of the Manifesto Writer; that did well enough as they were for the Doctor of Divinity. Neither is any reader in the world the less competent or likely to reap the less fruit of substantial learning from his reading for exercising his own judgment, and taking no author for infallible or entirely and in every thing to be relied on; but sifting what he reads and finding out not merely what was meant to be made known, but what was meant to be concealed. As perhaps he would be none the more competent nor ultimately the wiser for reading upon Dr. Smith's plan, of either swallowing all he reads without examination, or not suffering himself to see in what he reads, any thing that shall contravene his own conceit; and so setting bars against improvement by calling those who know no better than himself paragons of learning and "princes of critics;" and calling those who do know better, just what he pleases to call them.

SECTION VII.

LIBERTIES TAKEN WITH THE SCRIPTURES BY ERASMUS.

"For the book of Revelation, there was no original Greek at all, but Erasmus wrote it himself, in Switzerland, in the year 1516. — Bishop Marsh, vol. 1, page 320." — Manifesto.

1. "After what we have already seen, the reader will not be surprised at being assured that this also is a gross falsehood, and that the pretended reference to the learned bishop is another important forgery." Page 32.

No, indeed, the reader will not be surprised at any intensity of abuse, virulence of virtuperation, and excess of triumph, which this good Christian Divine would exhibit upon an unguarded position left to his conquest, after having exhausted the whole artillery of accusation without reaching the outermost lines of our defence. Not the shadow of a falsehood, not an iota of a forgery, has he yet discovered; and if that name, and no other, must be given to an INDEX *referring* to a fact and to the authority, where the fullest exposition of that fact would be found, because, from the extreme necessity of abbreviating its terms, it had abbreviated itself of some, that were absolutely necessary to its sense, or to its accuracy, but which would be supplied the moment the authority referred to was consulted ; yet, where certainly it is the only incorrectness, in cannot be called another forgery — where it is the first error, it cannot be *also* a falsehood — but —

If in the line "*for the Book of the Revelation there was no original Greek at all but Erasmus,*" &c., had been supplied the words, " FOR THE MOST ESSENTIAL PASSAGE IN THE BOOK OF REVELATION *there was no original Greek at all,*" — this filling up of the ellipsis absolutely necessary to the understanding of an INDEX, would have removed all ground of fair objection while it would hardly have led to any stronger impression of this monk's recklessness of truth and honesty than the passage as it stands imputes to him, and his whole character in life fully confirms. The passage which Erasmus thus audaciously interpolated and added of his own invented Greek to that which he represented as contained in his manuscript, contains the words, " If any man shall add unto these things, God shall add unto him the plagues that are written in this book," &c. This entire passage, from the 18th verse (Rev. xxii.) to the end, was first put forth to the world under a false pretence, and rested solely on the Greek which Erasmus had made from the Latin Vulgate. The reader might thus have been put in possession of a more explicit and I admit a more accurate statement; but the Manifesto instead of being an Index would have become a treatise; instead of referring the reader to the sources of more explicit information, it would have supplied that information itself — and its language, instead of being in every instance, *See there!* should have been, *See here!* — instead of its style running, "*If these things can be denied or disproved, your ministers and preachers are earnestly called on to do so!*" the reader would not have been surprised at being *assured* that it was the Index gave him to understand, and called upon to take the matter it only glanced at as truth, upon the only principle on which Dr. Smith's matter can be taken for truth, namely, looking no further into it.

Had no reference been given to have enabled the reader to acquaint himself more accurately with the matter referred to; or if, on referring to the works of that Bishop, no information on that subject was to have been found, the Manifesto certainly would have been chargeable with an air of dogmatism, and would, in this instance, have failed of the fidelity to be expected from every work of the character which it purports to sustain, which is, that of an Index Indicatorius; with which dogmatism is not chargeable — of which fidelity it hath not failed.

Let the reader glance his eye over the index to any great and extensive work: I know of none in which he shall not frequently and continually find, that when he turns to the matter which the index referred him to, it does not, upon that fuller explication, come up to the strength of the impression which the index had led him to expect; and here, after all, it is only the author's and the reader's *judgment* as to the matter that is at issue: and at the worst, the author has only used an ordinary method in calling attention to his labors, to provoke investigation, and to stimulate inquiry.

It is only one, who has as little respect for truth as he has for the decent courtesies of life, and the established allowances and deferences of the commonwealth of learning, that would, for any advantage that a detected error could give to his argumentation, violate the echoes of the grove with the eructation of the shambles and the gospel-shop.

An error is not a falsehood — a misquotation is not a forgery. But when it is for what in the very worst view was only an error — that we find that error called a *gross error* — when it is to that which is really no forgery at all we find the terms applied that it is " an impudent forgery," what can we say but that such a charge is a DOWNRIGHT *John Pye Smith:* a fair example of the manners, the style, and the conscience of a minister of the gospel — a preacher of salvation through blood, and — GO TO CHAPEL AND HEAR IT YOURSELVES!

Of the accuracy and fidelity of Erasmus, on whom the main chance for the accuracy and fidelity of all versions of the Greek Testament subsequently derived from his, must ultimately depend, we find from Marsh's Michælis, vol. 2, chap. xii, sect. 1, p. 444, edit. 3, London, 1819, (only Dr. Smith will assure the reader that this is another impudent forgery, for as in the Church of Rome, so among our no less priest-ridden *dissenters*, a man is not to believe his own eyes, nor trust his own reason in contradiction to God's ministers.) We find that there is a reading in the second Epistle to Peter (which Epistle itself is of questionable authenticity) which Erasmus has foisted in, which no one has been able to discover in any manuscript whatever. The word happens to be one of the most frightful significancy of the whole evangelical canonade — the war-whoop of the gospel, $\alpha\pi\omega\lambda\epsilon\iota\alpha\varsigma$. In the twenty-second chapter of the book of Revelation, he has even ventured to give his own translation from the Latin, because the Codex Reuchlini, which was the only Greek manuscript which he had of that book, was there defective. Of this, his only copy for so important a part of Scripture he boasted that it was " tantæ vetustatis ut apostolorum ætate scriptum videri potest," of such antiquity as to seem to have been written in the age of the apostles, though it contained internal evidence of the hand-writing of Andrew of Cæsarea, in the ninth century; and he himself borrowed it from Reuchlin, though it was not his property; but was borrowed by Reuchlin, from the monks of the Monastery of Basil; and he kept it himself for thirty years, till he died. Dr. Mill says, "that of a hundred alterations, which Erasmus made, in his edition of 1527, ninety relate to the Revelation only. One of his most violent opponents was the learned Spaniard Lopez de Stunica, who published 'Annotationes Adversus Erasmus in defensione translationis N. T.' Erasmus replied in his Apologies, both to him and his other antagonists; and the controversy has been thus far useful, that many points of criticism have been cleared up, which would otherwise have remained obscure. But the character of Erasmus seems to have lost by it, for he was more intent on his own defence than the investigation of truth." Vol. 2, p. 445.

What more to the just disparagement of this great man the Expositions of Lopez might have brought forward I have not here * the means of knowing, Though to hear both sides is the first maxim of reason and justice; yet it is a most certain and safe presumption that if he brought forward any thing like the language of Dr. John Pye Smith, Erasmus had no formidable opponent.

The writer of the Manifesto has now met the shock of the doctor's furious attack — Truth and not Victory, is his aim. That there should be nothing in the Manifesto that might have been worded better than it was, or that might

---

* Here in the Oakham Gaol, being a prisoner of Jesus Christ. Some apology I hope for the deficiency!

not fairly and justly be liable to censure and correction, (as I cheerfully admit this part of the Manifesto is,) — is what I never hoped; but that a single sentence of it should be liable to the charge of forgery or fraud, is what I never feared.

One single argument, that had been pregnant of such an inference, though couched in language of silk, and breathed in tones of music, I can tell this angry Doctor, would have been more terrible than all his foul, ill-mannered, and unmeasured revilings; and had he but shown in any one passage of his book, a capacity to perceive a truth that made against his own views, a disposition to recognize any one claim of his antagonist, on a humane or liberal consideration; his criticism would have been respectable, and his censure formidable. As it is, he perches but as a gnat upon a cow's horn; and God only knows, or cares, whether he intended to sting us, or to rest himself and be off again.

SECTION VIII.

THE ORIGIN AND CHARACTER OF THE TEXT, IN THE COMMON EDITIONS OF THE GREEK TESTAMNET.

1. "From the facts already stated, the impartial reader will be at no loss to judge concerning what this dishonorable Manifesto writer, chooses to call the infinitely suspicious origination of the present received text." I beg leave to suggest, that no impartial reader would *presume* the Manifesto writer to be dishonorable; that no

facts, already stated, support the presumption of dishonor, and that the reader has full right to retain his character of impartiality, even though he should not be content to acquiesce in the condemnation which either party may pronounce against the other.

2. "His parade of referring to the introduction of the Unitarian Improved Version, is in the same spirit of deception."

But there has been no deception in any part, in any iota of the Manifesto. Even in the instance in which the mighty effort made to compress immense extent of matter into the smallest compass of exhibition, has caused a syncopation or synechdoche which read as a detail, which it is *not* — rather than as an index referring to a detail, which it *is* — might lead to an *error*, there is no deceit, no intention of deceiving; the reader, referring to the given authority, will find the whole matter extensively set before him; and surely no writer intending to produce a false impression would have put into the hands of the reader the means of instantly correcting it.

3. "His parade of referring," &c., (p. 33,) coupled with the charge in his first paragraph of my "making an ostentatious reference to the titles of books, chapters, pages, and passages, marked as quotations, when the books and passages say no such thing;" are words which would surely lead the reader to understand that he had at least, some *one* or *two* palpable hits at the honor of the Manifesto writer, and that he had found a passage purporting to be in such a page of such an author, of which he could say, THESE WORDS ARE NOT THERE. But what is deceit? what is falsehood? and deceit and falsehood of the most malicious and evangelical character; if it be not, after such a force of accusation, to be obliged

to shirk off with the evasion that these words which are there quoted, are *garbled;* and that the quoter who quoted what served his own purpose, (which was certainly all that he intended to quote,) ought to have quoted something else, which would have served somebody else's purpose? I freely, and once for all, confess, that after many years of study and acquaintance with divines, and with their works, (and I wish I knew less of them than I do,) experience has shown me that their's is bad company, and that a man can make no better advantage of his misfortune in falling into it, than by informing himself, as an honest man would, of the mysteries of a gang of thieves, taking their word, not for all that they say, but for what they sometimes say without meaning that it should strike vulgar observance, when nature's honesty will, ever and anon, break out or press through the policy of the craft, and tell us unexpected truth.

With this view, and this alone, I quote Christian authors; and as the wicked murderer, in his sleep, betrays the secret of his burthened conscience in broken sentences, and unconcatenated ejaculations; in this way also, may more than divines meant to communicate, be extracted from their writings. And all the pledge for the fidelity of this most important of all possible exercises of critical shrewdness, is the proof that, say they whatever else they might say, contradict, recall, confuse, deny, confound; yet, *this,* which we present as their saying, is, what they really did say; of this, we produce the undeniable evidence; we claim no more privilege for our inference, than we yield to the most opposite inference and let the galled jade wince!

I did not quote the passage from the Unitarian Improved Version which my reverend opponent thinks I ought to have quoted, 1st. Because I did not believe it myself. I hope that may pass for *one* good reason; and 2dly, because it would have been utterly impossible to have made quotations of so great a length within the compass of space assigned to my whole matter; and *that* for another. But as for my being an " unprincipled slanderer and deceiver," I throw myself on the reader's justice to decide whether 'tis *my* character or his own that this meek and humble minister of Christ compromises, when, in the very volume which he accused me of having falsely pretended to quote, there, even in the same section that he himself was quoting; *there* before his eyes were the very sentences as purporting to be quoted by me: where he must have seen that they were *not* garbled nor put in stronger light than they would have appeared if read and connected together in the connection of the whole Dissertation from beginning to end, and standing thus within ten lines of the period which the doctor would have had me quoted.

" So THAT the received text rests upon the authority of no more than twenty or thirty manuscripts, most of which are of little note." Such, reader, is the whole of the sentence, thus exhibiting in itself a succinct and complete sense; and the only variation in the quotation as it stands in the Manifesto, is the omission of the two words, *So that*. The sentence which immediately follows in the Unitarian Version is, — " But since the received text was completed in the Elzevir edition of 1624, upwards of three hundred manuscripts either of the whole or of different parts of the New Testament, have been collated by learned men with much care, industry, and skill."— Introduct. page x.

From this sentence, marking it as the matter of a distinct sentence, I extracted so much of the information as

I wanted, adhering to the words as closely as possible in an abbreviation of them.

It *(i. e.* the received text,) was completed by the Elzevir edition of 1624.

Reader! without appealing to thy impartiality, I ask thy reason, I ask thine eyes, is this referring to the Unitarian Improved Version, in the spirit of deception; is this garbling; is this endeavoring to show a sense in a part of a sentence which the whole sentence taken together would not imply, or which the whole argument in which it stands, would be found to contravene? Or is it (of all men on earth,) for *him* to accuse another of garbling or quoting a passage deceitfully, who, at the very time, and in the very argument that he offers, to make it seem that another has done so, does so himself, and makes what the Unitarian Editors say of the books of the New Testament, pass for a refutation of what the writer of the Manifesto has said of the *Received Text* of the New Testament; which the Editors of the Unitarian Version were so far from intending to contravene, that they have actually said, not only all that the Manifesto said on that subject, but much more to the same purpose?

For what end, then, does the Reverend Doctor Smith apply such terrible epithets to the author of the Manifesto? Why thus call him an unprincipled slanderer and deceiver? Why, but to conceal his own machinations, to supply by clamor, the total want of argument; and to set pursuit on the wrong track by crying STOP THIEF! when all the while — aye! when all the while! — Oh, God! what a wicked world it is! — Surely, Dr. Smith ought to feel that the greatness of the occasion calls for his prayers — he shall have the full benefit of mine — God forgive him!

I shall now subjoin without note or comment, a few of the

ADMISSIONS OF THE MOST LEARNED CRITICS, AS TO THE INFINITELY SUSPICIOUS ORIGINATION OF THE RECEIVED TEXT —

Which the reader may, if he pleases, take Dr. John Pye Smith's word, are impudent forgeries and unblushing falsehoods, but which if he turns to the authors referred to, will be very likely to stare him in the face.

1. A. D. 1624. — An edition of the Greek Testament was published at Leyden, at the office of the Elzevirs, who were the most eminent printers of the time. The Editor, who superintended the publication is UNKNOWN. — Unit. Improved Version, Introduct. p. 9.

2. It does not appear that the editor was in possession of *any* manuscript. — Ibid.

3. This edition, however, being elegantly printed, &c., it was UNACCOUNTABLY TAKEN FOR GRANTED, that it exhibited a pure and perfect text. — Ibid.

4. THIS, constitutes the received text. — Ibid.

5. The early editors of the New Testament, possessed but *few* manuscripts, and those of *inferior* value. — Ibid. p. x.

6. Those of the Complutensian Editors were destroyed; but they were not numerous nor of great account. *

7. Erasmus consulted only five or six.

8. Robert Stephens, only fifteen.

9. They were collated, and the various readings noted, by Henry Stephens, the son of Robert, a youth about eighteen years of age. — Ibid. viii.

---

* I have shown however, (though it makes against my own argument,) that they were more respectable than the Unitarian Editors, or Bishop Marsh himself, at first apprehended them to be.

10. This book, being splendidly printed, with great professions of accuracy, by the Editor, was long supposed to be a correct and immaculate work. — Ibid.

11. It was published, A. D. 1550. — Ibid.

12. It differs very little from the received text. — Ibid.

13. It has been discovered to abound with errors. — Ibid.

14. Attempts have been make to correct the Received Text, by critical conjecture. — Ibid. p. xv.

15. The Orthodox charge the heretics with corrupting the text ; and

16. The Heretics recriminate upon the Orthodox. — Notes on Luke i. Unit. N. V. page 121.

17. The works of those writers who are called Heretics, such as Valentinian, Marcion, and others, are as useful in ascertaining the value of a reading, as those of the Fathers who are entitled Orthodox; for the Heretics were often more learned and acute and equally honest. — Introduct. p. xv.

18. For as yet (*i. e.* the fourth century,) there was no law enacted which excluded the ignorant and illiterate from ecclesiastical preferments and offices, and it is certain that the greatest part both of the bishops and presbyters, were men entirely destitute of learning and education. Besides,

19. That savage and illiterate party which looked upon all sorts of erudition, particularly that of a philosophical kind, as pernicious and even destructive of true piety and religion, increased both in number and authority. — Mosheim, vol. i, p. 346.

20. A l'égard du Nouveau Testament l'Hérésiarque (scil. Manichée), entreprit de le corriger, sous le frivole

prétexte, que les Evangiles n'étaient point des Apôtres, ni des hommes apostoliques dont ils portent les noms : ou que s'ils en étaient, ils avaient été falsifiés par des Chrétiens, qui étaient encore á demi juifs.

21. L'impartialité, si essentielle á un historien, m'a obligé de justifier les Manichéens de l'accusation que les Catholiques leur ont intentée, d'avoir corrumpu les livres du Nouveau Testament par des additions, ou des Retranchemens sacrilegés. Je l'ai examinée, et l'ai trouvée sans fondement. Mais je n'ai pû m'empêcher de remarquer à cette occasion, qu'il y eut des Catholiques assez téméraires pour ôter quelques endroits des Evangiles. — Beausobre, Histoire du Manichéisme, préface xi. à Amsterdam, 1734.

22. Si les hèrètiques ôtent un mot du texte sacrè, ou s'ils en ajoutent un, ce sont de sacrilèges violateurs de le sainteté des ècritures ; mais si les Catholiques le fout, cela s'appelle retoucher les premiers exemplaires, les réformer pour les rendre plus intelligibles. — Ibid, p. 343.

The reader will be pleased to observe, that the above is the passage in the text of Beausobre, upon which the statement about Lanfranc, in the Manifesto, is a note illustrative, which it was convenient for this Doctor of Divinity not to see, or, seeing which, it was convenient to his conscience to charge the Manifesto Writer with dishonesty for doing, what the Manifesto Writer was not doing, but what he was doing himself. — Steal! and cry *Stop thief!* is *gospel* all over!

23. The Latin version is the source of almost all European versions. — Marsh's Michælis, vol. 2. page 106.

24. No manuscript now extant is prior to the sixth century; and what is to be lamented, various readings which, as appears from the quotations of the fathers, were in the text of the Greek Testament, are to be found in

none of the manuscripts which are at present remaining. — Ibid. page 160.

This is but a spicilegium which the reader may safely multiply by a hundred, of the *gross forgeries*, and *no such passages*, and *no such things as are imputed to them*, but which *there*, in his face and in his teeth all the while, I might have obtruded on the angry Doctor's patience, in comprobation of the position of the Manifesto.

But the Manifesto is an index, not a dissertation, and enough was given there, as perhaps more than enough is given here, to prove, from the admissions of the most learned critics, the infinitely suspicious origin of the received text.

The claims of the scriptures, therefore, in any existing version of them, to resemblance or identity with their original, God only knowing what that original may have been, seems to be much in the same predicament as that of the Irishman's knife, which had unquestionably descended from the first king of Connaught, though it had had seventy thousand new blades, and fifty thousand new handles.

But to evade the pregnant conclusion of the matter which forces itself into his own reluctant admissions, the Doctor rings the changes again on his eternal sophism about the Greek tragedians and historians, as if it were proof enough for the claims of a divine revelation, to prove as much for it as can be proved for a pagan romance, or a barbarous melo-drame. We write better poems and more accurate histories, than any of the Hesiods or Homers, the Herodotuses, or Livys of antiquity — there is no Eschylus, Euripides, or Sophocles, that ever produced a play that would be endured in a British theatre, much less be worthy of an hour's study of the man who could read SHAKSPEARE! What are Virgil or Pindar to Byron and Moore? the man who had read Horace and the Iliad, might possibly attain the beauties of style and fervor of expression that appear in the Answer to the Manifesto — the man who had studied Shelley's Queen Mab would become a gentleman. After all that could be urged for the coequal claims of ancient poets, and as ancient evangelists, is *all* that can be urged, *enough*? or shall the ground which is solid enough to pitch a tent on be a sufficient foundation for a castle?

But surely, to argue that it is only of late years, and since the world has been blessed with the critical ingenuity and industry of a Mill, Wetstein, Griesbach, Middleton, Knapp, and Voter, that we are in possession of the correct, or *probably* correct text of Scripture, is little else than to transfer the authority of apostleship from the first writers to the modern critics. By the same argument it may be inferred, that *subsequent* critics may make subsequent discoveries, which may give us as good reason to alter the text from our *present* reading, as we have for holding the present reading at present the best. We do not arrogate to our own times an infallibility which we deny to others, when we presume to think that the text, as *we* have it, can be depended on, or that it may not be a thousand years to come, and after another hundred and thirty thousand various readings shall have been discovered, ere mankind shall have a right to felicitate themselves on reading a text in the closest accordance with the original.

But if we are to take the *knock-down dictum* of an insolent priest, who will call us "*obstinate untractable wretches*," for resisting his arguments! If we must, on the *ipse dixit* of a pretended prince of critics, believe that

"that text is competently exact even in the worst manuscript, nor is one article of faith or moral precept either perverted or lost in it," why there's an end on't! and what use of any other critic upon earth but he? What use of a revelation from God, when the prince of critics can brush up any dirty lumber into gospel, and give it with his "Take that, or BE DAMNED?" (Mark, xvi. 16,) or what use of any God on earth, when any canting fanatic, in the very slavering of *learned idiotcy*, shall be so ready and so able to officiate in his damnable capacity, to launch his curses, and denounce his vengeance?

SECTION IX.

IMMORAL TENDENCY OF THE SCRIPTURES.

1. "Here is, indeed, the highest pitch of daring."
"Here," (exclaims the doctor, in a strain that makes humanity hope his constitution may have no tendency to apoplexy) — "Here is the first born of calumny."
He might as well, however, have left it to his readers to determine whether the Manifesto demonstrates that its writer defies all truth and justice — for truth and justice will determine that however ill a man may think of his enemy, it is not his enemy's guilt that constitutes his innocence; nor is it the devil's blackness that makes an angel white.
2. "Study the passages to which he refers, in their respective connection, and in their relation to the other parts of the New Testament," says this learned Divine.

But *no!* say common sense and honesty. If a thing be apparently right and fair; if it be manifestly founded in reason — loyal, just, and pure — what occasion is there for study? Shall palpable villany, seen, caught, and held in the very act and article of crime, defeat our indignation, and bilk us into terms of peace, by the sophistical evasion — " You don't know me — you don't see the bearings and connections of the matter — study this part of my conduct, in relation to other parts of my conduct, and you will find it forms no exception to the SPOTLESS PURITY, the HOLY BEAUTY, which animates the whole of my divine composition. I pick a pocket, and I cut a throat, now and then! but how *unfair* to suspect my general character."

Will Dr. Smith show that there was, or could have been, any religion on the face of the earth, so vile and wicked, that it might not have been defended by precisely the same argument? Can the imposture of the Koran, the Shaster, the Vedas, the Pourannas, or any other pretended Divine Revelation, be pointed out by any fairer demonstration of the cheat, than that which should show, that amid all their pretended sanctities and sublimities — their spotless purity and their holy beauties — there were passages enough to be found in them to betray the craft which they originated, and the deceit which they intended? Might not the institutions of Lycurgus — the laws of Draco — or the bloody statute of Henry the Eighth, be vindicated upon the principle of " studying them all in the connections and relations that might be imagined to appertain to them," and explaining away the gross sense of the atrocities they contain, by taking *their own word* for the sincerity of the philanthropy they profess? Might not the language of Doctor John Pye Smith himself, be supposed to be such a gentleman and a scholar could have used, if we are obliged to give him credit either for the truth of his professions, or the sincerity of his motives?

The doctor himself admits that there are *difficulties* in the Bible, but seems incapable of the ingenuousness that should own, that those difficulties are difficult enough to appear to have an immoral, vicious, and wicked tendency, in which appearance all their difficulty consists. He begs off this by the complete surrender of putting the WORD OF GOD, on as good a footing as the fabulous legends of antiquity, and claiming that the same allowance should be made for the inspirations of infinite wisdom, as for the madrigals of Drunken Barnaby.

3. "The rational method of resolving them is by acquiring the information necessary to go to the bottom of each instance," says the doctor, (p. 27.) And so, 'tis the rational way to catch sparrows, to put a little salt upon their tails.

4. "And those who cannot do so, possess, in an enlightened Protestant country,"

Where's that?

5. "The inestimable advantage of consulting learned and judicious commentators."

But was not the advantage greater in a CATHOLIC country, of consulting commentators, who were not merely learned and judicious, but absolutely *infallible*, and who, when the difficulty was propounded to THEM, would have answered it perhaps, without giving you worse names than you might get from a Methodist parson, for your pains.

6. "With respect to the passages enumerated by this contemptible writer, a man must have little understanding indeed, whose careful examination cannot dissipate whatever of difficulty is pretended."

There reader! half of *that* is for yourself, for if your examination should not be careful *enough*, or should not lead to such a complete dissipation of the difficulty, as Dr. Smith opines must be its issue, he gives you hint enough that you shall be contemptible too.

7. " For, if the truth of God hath more abounded through my lie unto his glory, why yet am I also judged as a sinner?" Rom. iii, 7. How this can be the language of an objector, and not the Apostle's own language, an apostle only can show us. How its most frightful and revolting sense — which is at least the apparent one, is incompatible with the character of one who calls himself "*the chief of sinners*," and who calls the other apostles, "false apostles, dogs, and liars;" or how it is relieved — by apposition with innumerable other texts of the same epistoler, to the full effect of representing the God of truth and mercy, as the greatest monster of iniquity — " giving up his creatures to vile affections and a reprobate mind, that he might have mercy on whom he would have mercy, and whom he would, might harden;" — how this can be compatible with holy beauty, or reconciled to moral justice, they only can show who can show falsehood and forgery in the Manifesto, and prove that the pitch of Vulcan's smithy, was whiter than the pearl on Juno's coronet.

8. " If there come any unto you and bring not this doctrine, receive him not into your house, neither bid him God-speed, for he that biddeth him God-speed, is partaker of his evil deeds." John ii. 10. This text, says our all-explaining doctor, " forbids the aiding and encouraging of corrupt and wicked teachers, but it does not forbid any acts of humanity or civility towards them as our fellow creatures."— (p. 7.)

The devil it doesn't! A word with you, Doctor, if you please! How were the learners to know that the teachers were corrupt before they had learned what it was that the teachers had to teach? And if the learners themselves actually knew best, how could they have any teachers at all? or what was the depth of that learning whose nature could be fairly judged of sooner than you could say, *How d'ye do*? Or if these questions savor of levity — imagine a more serious one if you can, than the question whose emergence from your own position cannot be evaded, and imagine, if you can, an answer to it.

If, before that epistle itself was written — if *there* and *then*, in the Apostolic age, while the beloved John, the centre and source of orthodoxy, was living and basking under the plenary illapses of inspiration, false teachers, and corrupters of the Christian doctrine were so rife, that Christians had to live upon the *snap* to keep the gospel-preaching vagabonds out of their houses: how are we to be sure, that in the course of eighteen hundred years, false teachers haven't smuggled themselves into good livings, and brought in the vilest trash that was ever foisted on the credulity of a choused and insulted people? Especially considering, that what our teachers tell us is so pure and holy, smells so rank and KNOCK-YE-DOWN in such a many places, and cost a man such a head-ache before he can dissipate the effect of the first *haut-goat*, and swallow in all, as a lump of spotless purity and holy beauty! But "*shut your eyes and open your mouth, and see what God will send you,*" is the divinity of the college, as well as of the nursery; the only difference being, that there is an air of sportive innocence and joke in the game of the little ones, while the game, as played by the grown babies, is not innocent, and is no joke!

9. "To persecution, in every form and degree," says the Doctor, " the whole spirit of the Gospel is entirely opposed." N. B. — Only a little private assassination now and then, is recommended. Acts vi.; Corinth. i. 15.; Galat. v. 12.

10. " The words of Heb. xii, 22. 'Our God is a consuming fire,' are figurative language, borrowed from the Sublime Diction, &c., and every school-boy knows that the word HATE or *hatred*, denotes no malevolent disposition, but only that holy heroism of virtue." * — (p. 37.) Go it, Dr. Smith; at this rate how easy is the business of explanation! — the Persian shall supply thee with the literal text of his creed, the very words of his holy liturgy, than which he could use no other to express his sincere idolatory of FIRE — the Cannibal shall hand over to thee all the modes of expression by which he indicates and *means* his feast on human flesh, and thou wilt explain it all to some high sense of mystical holiness. Cannibalism shall be spotlessly pure; malevolence shall be heroism, and consuming fire shall be a fit metaphor for a God of mercy.

11. You offer in illustration of the dispositions produced by Christianity, the conduct of the Bavarian martyr. Here, Sir! you are not to be misunderstood; here you stand committed, and in the contemplation of this frightful instance, you are no more to be dealt with by the mild censure of the critical diasurmus and the sufficient castigation of merited ridicule; but the sense of your deluded and insulted readers must be aroused to a perception of

---

* In like manner, as every school-boy knows, that no falsehood, however apparent and palpable it may be, denotes falsehood when the parson tells it.

the precipice of horrors, to which, either in the error of your ignorance, or of your madness, you would lead them.

Persuade the babes and sucklings of the Gospel, that I am all that malice could conceive me to be — feed them with the pure milk of your word for it — that the Author of the Manifesto must needs be all that your coarse mind could think, and all your coarse language could call him — you have not yet approached the showing evidence, that he had renounced the *profession* of something moral and virtuous — you have not yet pourtrayed him as that monstrous suicide — that rebel against nature — that enemy of his own flesh — that unnatural father — that merciless husband — that wretch, immoveable by a child's tears, unconquerable by a woman's love; that — nothing that was man — that scandal of humanity — that thief of man's face,

> "———— On foreign mountains bred,
> Wolves gave him suck, and savage tigers fed."

Your BEAVARIAN MARTYR! Take him, crown him with your laurels, cover him with your honors, exhibit him as the creature, the production, the model of Christianity, and say, *See here!* I will say, see here, too; and when you shall have exalted your paragon to a Divinity, he shall serve me too, as the very instance that I would produce in exemplification of the character of a FIEND; and of the mischievous, demoralizing, and denaturalizing influence of that accursed superstition which alone could have produced so foul a monster — alone have formed your Bavarian martyr. If thou hast nature in thee, reader, bear it not! If nature be not wrong, say not that this could have been right. Imagine that thou hadst been the son or daughter of such a father, the wife of such a husband, and with all the possible sense of duty and affection of the one, with all the passionate devotion of the other — hadst been an infidel, (an imagination which Christians never trust themselves to imagine, a case with which they have no sympathies,) think, then, what a hell of domestic misery must the disposition of such a parent have caused — what compassion couldst thou have hoped to engage from the wretch that had no mercy on himself? What power of remonstrance could have prevailed over one whose inexorability of purposes would not yield to the argument of fire and death? What greater degree of obstinacy in a creature conscious of his liability to error, and compassed with infirmities? Let such a monster's madness take but another cue, and he would be as eager to inflict as he was obdurate to suffer. If such are the examples that Dr. John Pye Smith preaches at Homerton, it cannot be safe to sleep in that neighborhood. If such are the characters he commends, his foul language and his bitterest criminations are the highest compliment that he can pay: consummate vice, with him, is glorious virtue, and 'tis only his *good word* that could be injurious to any man.

12. Of the passages which betray a comparatively modern character,* of which the Manifesto gives six, out

---

* See a most ample store, illustrated with irresistable demonstrations of their modernism, in Evanson's Dissonance of the Four generally received Evangelists, which, as this divine, though of the Unitarian school, professed himself a sincere believer in Divine Revelation, have that additional weight which I have invariably brought to all my arguments — that of being concessions of the adverse party.

Mat. xix. verse 12, delivers the peculiar docterine of the En-

of six hundred which critical investigation might have adduced : the Doctor, with that priestly subtlety which

---

cratites, a sect which appeared very early in the second century. — Evanson, p. 168.

Matt. xvi. verse 18. — Matt. xviii. verse 17. The word church is used, and its papistical and infallible authority referred to as then existing, which is known not to have existed till ages after.

Matt. xi. verse 12. — From the days of John the Baptist until now, the kingdom of heaven suffereth violence, &c., could not have been written till a very late period.

Luke ii. verse 1, shows, whoever the writer was, he lived long after the events he related. His dates — about the fifteenth year of Tiberius, and the government of Cyrenius — the only indications of time in the New Testament, are manifestly false.

See references in the Epistles *to saints*, a religious order, owing its origin to the Popes. References to the distinct orders of Bishops, Priests, and Deacons, and calls to a monastic life, to fasting,, &c.

" In my Father's house are many *monasteries*" — so it should have been translated. — John xiv. 2.

"When we pray, don't speak like Battus," (Matt. vi. 7.) so it should have been translated, Battus being a talkative and foolish poet, as modern as you please.

See the words for legion, aprons, handkerchiefs, centurion, &c., in the original, not being Greek, but Latin, written in Greek characters, a practice first to be found in the historian Herodian, in the third century. — Evanson, p. 30.

The general ignorance of the four Evangelists, not merely of the geography and statistics of Judea, but even of its language — their egregious blunders, which no writers who had lived in that age could be conceived to have made, prove that they were not only on such persons as those who have been willing to be deceived, have taken them to be, but that they were not Jews — had never been in Palestine, and neither lived in or at any time near to the times to which their narratives seem to refer. The ablest German divines have yielded thus much ; the English reader will see it irrefutably proved by the Unitarian Evanson ; and the Latin scholar will find the argument, as far as it applies to the Gospel of St. John, in particular, cautiously, but convincingly handled, in the Probabilia of

characterizes his performance, skirks the great knot by the wheedling finesse of saying, that " the greater part present

---

Bretschneider, in which he modestly attempts to show that the author of that Gospel was no party or cotemporary of the events to which it relates, and neither a Jew, nor at any time an inhabitant of Palestine.

" Si forte accidisset ut Johannis evangelium per octodecim secula priora prorsus ignotum jacuisset et nostris demum temporibus in oriente repertum, et in medium productum esset, omnes haud dubie uno ore confiterentur Jesum a Joanne descriptum longe alium esse ac illum Matthæi, Marci et Lucæ; nec utramque descriptionem simul, veram esse posse." — Page 1. Modeste subjecit Carolus Theoph. Bretschneider, &c., Lipsiæ, 1820.

Indeed, the modernism of some of the passages in the epistles is truly ludicrous, and needs but a moment's reflection to detect the absolute impossibility of its having been written, or the like of such a thing having been imagined, in the imaginary apostolic age. Such is the passage, for quoting which, in its evident and inevadeable sense, as a part of the blasphemy of which I have been convicted, I am now a prisoner, 2 Cor. iii. verse 6. — " Who also hath made us able ministers of the New Testament; not of the letter, but of the spirit; for the letter killeth, but the spirit giveth life." If the reader can reconcile such a passage to any supposable circumstances or condition of a *first* preacher of the Gospel, ere yet any part of the New Testament was put into letter, his faith will remain unshaken.

Our English version egregiously protestantizes, whereby the really monkish character of the original is concealed from vulgar suspicion. One of the ten reasons which Chillingworth gives for turning Papist was, " Because the Protestant cause is now, and hath been from the beginning, maintained with gross falsifications and calumnies, whereof the prime controversy writers are notoriously, and in a high degree guilty." — See his Ten Reasons.

BRETSCHNEIDER. — It is to be regretted, that this work has not yet appeared in an English translation. The Germans seem far to have out-run us in the march of general scepticism. I have not quoted this work, however, without having duly weighed the answer to it in the same language, by the learned STEIN, of Branden-

no difficulty to an *intelligent* and *reflecting* reader —and of the others, a rational solution may be found by referring to any good commentator, such as Whitby, Doddridge, Scott, &c., and, (HEAR! READER! HEAR!) if there were no such passages, one great argument in favor of the genuineness of the scriptures would be wanting." (p. 38.)

By my honor, as pretty a bit of logic that as ever was conned. I prithee, reader, look back on it, and digest the knowledge thou hast gained.

Imprimis. — The position of the Manifesto, that there are innumerable passages in the New Testament which betray a comparatively modern date, is a false pretence; *nevertheless*, there are passages which do betray a modern date. *Nevertheless*, if the greater part of these present any difficulty to thee, thou art not an intelligent and reflecting reader. *Nevertheless*, thou shall find a rational solution of the difficulty in D'Oyley, and Mant, Clark, Williams' *Cottage* Bible, and others. And to crown all this vast accession to thy knowledge, thou shalt *nevertheless* conclude, like a thorough Three-one, One-three Trinitarian, that the marks of a very modern date are one of the clearest proofs of very high antiquity: just as thou wouldst know a poem to have been certainly written in the age of Shakspeare, and probably by Shakspeare himself, from the allusion that it contained to the battle of Waterloo, to gas-lights, and to steam-packets. Indeed, if there were no such allusions, one great argument in favor of the genuineness of the poem would be

---

burgh, i. e. *Authentia Evangelii Johannis Vindicata.* Stein's principal argument for the genuineness of this Gospel, seems to be the *experience* of a certain pious soldier, alias a Christian blood-hound, who found it particularly comfortable to his soul in the field of battle. Socrates must be silent when Xantippe RAVES.

wanting; and so, of course, the more the better. And the clearer proofs there are of forgery and imposture in these writings, the stronger will be the faith of the Christian in their genuineness and authenticity. Go it, Doctor! but what a pity that men who have learned to argue in this way, should ever have separated themselves from that Holy and Apostolic Roman Church, from whom not only their creed, but their logic is derived.

13. The passage from Rousseau is fairly and honorably quoted, and served effectually to the full stress for which it is quoted, and *valeat quantum valero potest*. But surely, when these good Christian divines argue, as we admit they do, very fairly, from concessions and admissions that have here and there dropped from the pens of infidels, and take no notice of such parts of their writings as they very well know would contravene, neutralize, or entirely destroy the effect of those admissions; they can have no right to complain at having this fair card played back upon themselves. We can make all that a Rosseau, a Chubb, or a D'Alembert may have yielded to Christianity kick the beam, with the plump-dead weight in the other scale of the scepticism of a Lardner, the deism of a Locke, and the materialism of a Tillotson.

For the proper understanding of the works of divines, even from the writings of those who are entitled to be considered as respectable, down to such as by the stupidity of their argumentation, and the scurrility of their language, show that they have renounced all claim to such a consideration; the *look-out* of the inquirer after truth should not be, not for what they wished to set before his observance, but for what they would fain should escape it — not for what they meant to say — but for what they did not mean to say.

SECTION X.

OF THE PROTOTYPES, OR FIRST SPECIMENS, AND ORIGINALS OF THE GOSPELS.

1. "THE Manifesto Writer, with his usual despite of truth and knowledge, speaks of true and genuine gospels of the most primitive Christians, and which he says have been rejected without any assignable reason, or alleged authority."

Then follows the Rev. Doctor's characteristic virulence of abuse, with which by this time, one might hope even dissenterian rancor would be satisfied.

Let Dector Pye Smith retain his unenvied laurels, and surpass all Wapping in the use of the vulgar tongue — let him stand the *Chrichton* of a style that no gentleman could have used and no scholar would have needed; I only wish the reader to give the utmost possible weight of consideration to the admissions made by the reverend gentleman himself, and which his extreme ferocity of language seems purposely adopted to screen from observation. There are, it seems, admissions which must be admitted, concessions which must be conceded; and therefore, that observance may not arrest them, that inference may not overtake them, there was no better policy than giving them their chance to escape in a tumult of tempestuous rage; but should the reader preserve his coolness, and retain composure of mind enough to ask, "What has he here?" he will not pay for another quarter's sitting in a dissenterian chapel, till he can find some more satisfactory way of solving his doubts, than calling the man an impudent liar who suggested them.

1. CONCESSION.—There were other narratives of the doctrines and adventures of Christ and his Apostles besides those which have come down to us.

INFERENCE. — And therefore could not be corruptions of the Gospels which have come down to us — but,

2. CONCESSION.—These narratives were earlier in time than those which have come down to us.

INFERENCE. — The Gospels which have come down to us might be the improvements, or last castigated and enlarged editions of these.

3. CONCESSION. — Those narratives of the life and actions of Jesus Christ were *fictitious*.

INFERENCE. — How know ye that?

4. CONCESSION. — They were written by many silly and fraudulent persons.

INFERENCE. — Who is it that gives them that character? and what better are your Evangelists?

5. CONCESSION. — By far the larger part of these have long ago dropped into *merited* oblivion.

INFERENCE. — Then, by what right can any one *now* take upon himself to say, that that oblivion was merited?

6. CONCESSION. — That they ever existed is known only from the records of the early Christian writers, usually called the Fathers.

INFERENCE. — 1. Such an assertion would do to be foisted on the bigotted Papist, who never reads the Scriptures, or on the no less bigotted fanatical dunce, who reads them in faith and prayer, and so is none the wiser for his reading. An intelligent and shrewd noticer of what he reads, would find, that he did not want the Fathers to have given him information of the existence of Gospels and narratives of the life and doctrines of

Christ, of rival pretensions, and unquestionably of earlier date, than any of the Scriptures which those good Fathers have suffered to come down to us.

2. He will find too, that "fictitious, silly, fraudulent, and deserving of oblivion," as those writings, now that their merits cannot be investigated, are assumed to be, it was certainly those writings that formed the faith of the first Christians, before *any* of the writings which form our New Testament were in existence.

3. He will find that the New Testament makes over all its authority to them — and

4. Ascribes to them the inspiration, sanctity, and sufficiency, which those who know nothing about them preposterously ascribe to the New Testament.

5. He will find that they are expressly quoted in the New Testament, and quoted as a source of appeal and higher authority recognized by the writers of the New Testament themselves.

6. He will find that the writers of the New Testament never presume to put their writings on a footing of equality with those earlier and more authentic narratives, but offer their compositions only as commentaries or sermons on the already established Holy Scripturess. For example, Timothy, when himself old enough to be Bishop of Crete, is said to have learned from his grandmother, Lois, and his mother, Eunice, (2 Tim. i. 5.) the Scriptures which were able to make him wise unto salvation, through faith, in Christ Jesus. (2 Tim. iii. 15.) And Luke expressly prefaces what has, by a shameful perversion, been called *his* Gospel, with a disclaimer of all pretence to co-equal authority with the then well-known and long established narratives of Christ and his exploits, but offers all he has to offer, as an avowed Family Expositor, having no author-

ity itself, but setting forth the certainty of those things in which the most excellent Theophilus had already been instructed.

7. He will find that had the text of the New Testament been fairly and ingenuously printed, so as to mark in CAPITAL LETTERS the words which stand for the titles of books, a glance of the eye would distinguish a CATALOGUE, of which I myself have counted upwards of a hundred and eighty, whose divinity and inspiration must be admitted, if there *now* are, or ever were in the world, any writings that had a claim to be considered as inspired and divine.

8. He will find, in like manner, that had the passages in the New Testament, which really are quotations from those apocryphal writings, being printed in *italics*, or marked with inverted commas, so as to indicate their *quoted* character, there are a great many more of them than have been ordinarily recognized; and that far higher honor and respect were paid and intended by the New Testament writers, to those (in their esteem) true and genuine Gospels, upon which *their* compositions are but commentaries.

9. He will find, too, that the method of distinguishing TITLES OF BOOKS, names of persons, and other important matters, which the sense required, should be so distinguished, with some difference in the manner of writing, and of marking quotations, as quotations, not having come into use till comparatively modern times, is the evident cause why the original authorities of many ancient books have come to be entirely lost sight of, and so surreptitious and plagiary copies, which I hold all the books of the New Testament to be, have come in time to supersede the use, and run away with the honors of those which were really the originals.

10. He will observe, too, that added to the fact, that the method of distinguishing titles of books, and quotations from those books, by a difference in the manner of writing, had not come into use when the books of the New Testament were compiled; the very fame, renown, and common notoriety of the unquestionable and unapproachable superiority of those then received and established rules of faith, are sufficient to account for the writers of the New Testament blending them with their own compositions as they have done, without any particular indications of quotation, — and nothing is more common now, even since we have adopted the method of distinguishing quoted sentences, than to consider the well-known style of a popular author as a sufficient excuse for not doing so; and so bringing in the sentiment and expression of a Shakspeare or of a Pope, as if it had

" Grown with our growth, and strengthened with our strength."

had been the original conception of our own minds, and had occurred as the most easy and natural way of rounding a period unmixed with baser matter.

As to the argument from the quotations of the writings of the New Testament to be met with in the writings of the early Fathers, and our obligations to *them*, for letting us know that " silly, fraudulent, and fictitious narratives of the life and actions of Jesus Christ and his Apostles ever existed," there happen to be just these fifteen following difficulties standing in the way of the conclusion to which Dr. Smith would marshal us, and standing, too, in the stubborn attitude of unyielding and unconquerable facts.

1. The same Fathers who quote, or seem to quote the writings contained in the New Testament, do also quote

those silly, fictitious, and fraudulent narratives, and that too, with quite as much respect and reverence, as they do the writings which are now deemed canonical.

2. The earlier the Fathers are in respect of time, the more frequent are their respectful and honorable references to the apocryphal, and the less their notice of the canonical Scriptures.

3. It is by no means ascertainable when the Fathers seem to quote passages from the New Testament, that it really was the New Testament which they quoted, and not those earlier and original writings of which the New Testament is only the compilation.

4. *Irenæus*, in the second century, is the first of the Fathers who, though he has no where given us as professed catalogue of the books of the New Testament, intimates that he had received four Gospels, as authentic Scriptures, the authors of which he describes.

5. But the same Father still retains the earlier and apocryphal writings, even the most silly of them, as of equal, and even paramount authority to the four Gospels, and gives the most silly and contemptible reasons: " Quare non sint plura nec pauciora quam quantuor Evangelia. — *Fabricius, Codex Apoc.* page 382, vol. 1, Hamburgh.

6. Origen, in the third century, an Egyptian priest, distinguished for folly beyond all names of folly, who died about the year 253, is the first writer who has given us a perfect catalogue of those books which Christians unanimously (or at least the greater part of them) have considered as the genuine and divinely inspired writings of the Apostles. — Introd. to the Critical Study and

Knowledge of the Holy Scriptures, by Thomas Hartwell Horne, vol. 1, p. 90.*

7. But Origen also quotes other and earlier writings, as of equal or paramount claims to those of the New Testament.

8. He admits, that if he should only relate those things which had fallen within the compass of his own knowledge, he should furnish infidels with abundant matter of laughter. — Chap. 39, *adverses Celsum* — and

9. That there are some ARCANA IMPERII, or secrets in the management, which are not fit to be communicated to the vulgar. — Chap. 8, *adversus Celsum*.

10. It is certain, that those whom their adversaries called HERITICS, from the very first retained those writings which the others rejected, challenged for them the

---

* Though Irenæus, in the second century, is the first who mentions the Evangelists, and Origen, in the third century, is the first who gives us a catalogue of the books contained in the New Testament, Mosheim's frightful admission stands still before us, in all the horrors of the inferences with which it teems. We have no grounds of assurance that the mere mention of the names of the Evangelists by Irenæus, or the arbitrary drawing up of a particular catalogue by Origen, were of any authority. It is still, unknown BY WHOM, or WHERE, or WHEN, the canon of the New Testament was settled. But in this absence of positive evidence we have abundance of negative proof. We know when it was *not* settled. We know that it was not settled in the time of the Emperor Justinian, nor in the time of Cassiodorius; that is, not at any time before the middle of the sixth century, "by any authority that was decisive and universally acknowledged; but Christian people were at liberty to judge for themselves concerning the genuineness of writings proposed to them as apostolical." — Lardner, vol. 3, pp. 54, 61. And certain it is, that the very earliest Fathers acted precisely upon the principle of our reverend Doctor; in the very act of charging others with forgery, which they could not prove, they were doing it themselves all the while, which could be proved.

higher and original authority, and rejected the compilations that were afterwards fraudulently foisted upon the people, by the power of the bishops, who happened to get the upper hand in the scramble — and

11. "It is an undoubted fact, that the heretics were in the right in many points of criticism, where the Fathers accused them of wilful corruption." — Bp. Marsh, vol. 2, p. 362. * — and

12. Were vastly more intelligent and learned — and

13. Vastly more candid, conscientious, and heedful of truth.

14. The inquirer will find, that the supreme and *exclusive* pretensions to divine inspiration and authority, now set up for the writings contained in the canonical scriptures of the Old and New Testament in particular, are a *surprisingly modern* trick — a new shuffle in the game of priestcraft; for, in reading the writings of the Fathers, even down to the Fathers of the English church, and the Homilies of the Church of England, set forth in the reign of Edward the Sixth, and renewed and enlarged by Elizabeth, as proper "to be *understanded* by the people," (Article 35.) he will find the works even of Socrates and Virgil, quoted as of divine inspiration, and the story of Toby and the Fish, or the Angel and the Dog, expressly ascribed to the Holy Ghost.†

15. He will find, that a really learned man, the very

---

* Yet ἰωδη βιβλια, "*poisonous books*," and δαιμονιωδη βιβλια "*devilish books*," were the best terms in which the orthodox could speak of writings which the heretics ascribed to Christ and his Apostles. The anger which they excited, is itself a demonstration that — there was SOMETHING in them.

† My copy of the Homilies is the Oxford Clarendon press, 8vo. I page from that edition :

"The meaning, then, of these sayings in the scriptures, and *other*

high and respectable authority which the Rev. Doctor John Pye Smith has referred to on this difficult subject, instead of assuming the tone and language of Dr. Smith, against those who most strenuously opposed him, modestly and generously admits, that, "In order to establish the canon of the New Testament, it is of absolute necessity that the pretences of all other books to canonical authority, be first carefully examined and refuted."—Jones on the Canon, &c., vol. 1, p. 23.

And, " for my own part, (says he) I declare, with many learned men, that in the whole compass of learning, I know no question involved with more intricacies and perplexing difficulties than this."—Vol. 1. p. 2.

How much obliged would this great man have been to Dr. Smith, for relieving him of his perplexities — by telling him that the pretences of all other books to canonical authority, were *shallow pretences*, and that, dissatisfied as he acknowledges himself to be with the result of his investigations, and apparently overwhelmed with a sense of their intricacies and perplexing difficulties, he had " put all question about them at rest for ever." (41.)

What a pity that he never thought of adopting Dr. Smith's way of putting a question to rest, by at once

---

holy writings, is, &c., (p. 330.) And St. Paul himself declareth, &c., &c. Even as Saint Martin said, &c. (82.) As the word of God testifieth, &c."— then followeth a passage, neither in the Old or New Testament. (205.) " As he saith in Virgil. (251.) As Seneca saith. (251.) As saith Saint Bernard."

All these authorities, taken together — the homily takes them together, with, " Thus have ye heard declared unto you what God requires by his word." And again, " The same lesson doth the Holy Ghost teach in sundry places." But not one of those sundry places is to be found in any part of the canonical scriptures.

calling those who made any question of the matter, unprincipled and impudent liars.

As for the reprinting of Jones' translations, without any acknowledgment of the authority from which they were taken, one would think that the evangelical Doctor had laid his charges thick enough upon me, without fathering me with a fogery and disingenuousness, if such he hold it to be, which is purely and entirely Christian. Hone's apocryphal New Testament, as it is called, being as he declared to me, compiled with no intention of discrediting the received Scriptures; and *Hone* himself being professedly a firm believer in Divine Revelation. *

In the works of Toland, the reader will find a much longer catalogue of apocryphal books than are noticed either in the Latin of John Albert Fabricius, or in the English of the fair and ingenuous Mr. Jeremiah Jones. To both their catalogues, as referring only to apocryphal scriptures of inferior claim, I here subjoin a list of the *apparent* titles of holy books, referred to in the New Testament itself, and therefore, with whatever contempt they may be spoken of, now that they are irrecoverably lost, by those who would not let the New Testament itself speak a language that did not harmonize with their hypothesis; they certainly were of higher antiquity, and of better evidence than any which the New Testament contains.

---

* Hone, however, might have availed himself of Archbishop Wake's translation.

IMPRIMIS. — TWENTY-SIX GOSPELS.

The Gospel of the Kingdom	Matt. xxiv. 14.
The Gospel by Christ himself.	Luke xx. 1.
The Gospel of God	1 Pet. iv. 15.
The Gospel to the Poor	Luke iv. 18.
The Gospel to the Dead*	1 Pet. iv. 6.
The Gospel of Christ	1 Gal. 7.
Another Gospel, which is not another †	1 Gal. 6.
The Gospel of Peace	Ephes. vi. 15.
The Gospel of Salvation	Ephes. i. 13.
The Gospel of Glory	2 Cor. iv. 4.
The Gospel to the Samaritans	Acts viii. 25.
The Gospel to Abraham	Gal. iii. 8.
The Gospel of the Blessed God	1. Tim. i. 11.
The Gospel of the Circumcision	Gal. ii. 7.
The Gospel of the Uncircumcision	Gal. ii. 7.
The Gospel which was preached unto every creature under heaven	Col. i. 23.
The Gospel which was preached privately to them that were of Reputation. ‡	Gal. ii. 2.

---

* The GOSPEL TO THE DEAD, or OF the dead, is unquestionably that which Christ was believed to have preached to the spirits in prison, and from some legend of which is derived that most important article in the Apostles' Creed — HE DESCENDED INTO HELL, the baptismal formulary of which is, THAT HE WENT DOWN INTO HELL, of which no trace is to be found in either of the four Gospels.

† Several instances of this rhetorical solecism are to be found in scripture, e. g. Deut. xxviii. 68, Ye shall be sold unto your enemies, for bondmen, and no man shall buy you. Luke ix. 18. And it came to pass, that when he was all alone, behold his disciples were with him.

‡ Query. Was there no trick in this private preaching?

The Gospel of Paul	Rom. ii. 16.
The Gospel of Paul, and Silvanus, and Timotheus	2 Thes. i. 10.
The Gospel of Jesus Christ . . .	Mark i. 1.
The Gospel of the Grace of God .	Acts xx. 24.
The Everlasting Gospel . . .	Rev. xiv. 6.
The Dispensation of the Gospel .	1 Cor. ix. 17.
The Faith of the Gospel . . .	Phil. i. 27.
The Mystery of the Gospel . . .	Col. i. 26.
The Truth of the Gospel . . .	Col. i. 5.

TWELVE WORDS, OR INSPIRED DISCOURSES.

The Word of the Lord . .	John xii. 48. / Acts xiii. 4
The Word of Christ	Col. iii. 16.
The Words of the Lord Jesus .	Acts xx. 35.
The Word of God	Rom. x. 17.
The Word of Life . . .	Phil. ii. 16. / 1 John i. 1.
The Word of Truth	Col. i. 5.
The Word spoken by Angels . .	Heb. ii. 2.
The Word of Righteousness . .	Heb. v. 13.
The Word of Faith . . .	Rom. x. 8.
The Words of Salvation . . .	Acts xiii. 26.
The Mass and Liturgy of Faith .	2 Phil. xvii. 30

Θυσια και λειτουγια. Such are the original words — it was good Protestantism to translate them into the less *tell-tale* form of the SACRIFICE and SERVICE of your faith. By a similar manœuvre of good Protestantism, the English reader is put off the scent of tracing the monkish origin of John xiv. 2. "In my father's house are many monasteries," εν τη οικια του πατρος μου μοναι πολλαι εισιν by finding the word μονη, of which the Latin significations are, mansio, quies, desidia, mora, monasterium, translated into mansion, which signifies rather a palace or public residence, than a *solitude*, which the root from which the word is derived indicates, and which the context supports — *I go to prepare a place for you.*

12. The Traditions of the Apostles . 2 Thess. iii, 6.

FIVE TESTIMONIES.

The Testimony of God . . .	1 Cor. ii. 1.
The Testimony of Christ . . .	1 Cor. i. 6.
The Testimony of Jesus . . .	Rev. i. 9.
The Testimony of our Lord . .	2 Tim. i. 8.
The Testimony of Paul and Sylvanus, and Timotheus	2 Thess. i. 10.

The reader must not think that because the subjects of the books were the same, the books were identical. The variation of a syllable or of the singular for the plural number, in the title of books is sufficient to indicate that they had different authors: and when we *know* the fact that different authors had written on the subject or theme of Christianity, even that "MANY had taken in hand to set forth," &c., before any one of our received Gospels can be dated; not having the names of the authors themselves, we can only distinguish one of these from another by those variations which would naturally occur in the different titles, which different authors would give to their different accounts of the same general story — one calling his "the Testimony of, or concerning Christ," another designating his "the Testimony of, or concerning Jesus," or a "Discourse or Word of the Lord Jesus," or "Word or Doctrine of Jesus Christ," &c., &c.

SIXTEEN MYSTERIES.

The Mystery of the Kingdom . . Mark iv. 11.
The Mystery of the Gospel . . . Col. i. 26.
The Mystery of God . . . . . Col. ii. 2.
The Mystery of Christ . . . Ephes. iii. 4.
The Mystery of the Woman . . Rev. xvii. 7.
The Mystery of the Seven Stars . Rev. i. 20.
The Mystery which had been hid from ages . . . . . . Col. i. 26.

---

* "Stewards of the mysteries of God," 1 Cor. iv. 1, is the title which Paul arrogates to himself and his colleagues in imposture — the very identical and unaltered title of the Pagan Hierophants — privy counsellors of God! Luke viii. 10. "Unto you it is given to know the mysteries of the kingdom of God; but to others in parables, that seeing, they might not see; and hearing, they might not understand." Luke vii. 22. "To the poor the Gospel is preached."

"The profound respect that was paid to the Greek and Roman mysteries, &c., induced the Christians to give their religion a *mystic air*, in order to put it upon an equal footing, in point of dignity, with that of the Pagans." — Mosheim, vol. 1, p. 204. "They used in the celebration of the sacrament, several of the terms employed in the heathen *mysteries*, and adopted the rites and ceremonies of which these renowned mysteries consisted." — Ibid. "He hath instituted and ordained holy mysteries, as pledges of his love," &c. "Consider the dignity of that holy mystery, and the great peril of the unworthy receiving thereof." — Exhortations in Liturgy. If the reader cannot draw the necessary inference, his faith will remain unshaken.

The Mystery of Godliness	1 Tim. iii. 16.
The Mystery of Iniquity	2 Thess. ii. 7.
The Mystery of Faith	1 Tim. iii. 9.
The Wisdom of God in a Mystery	1 Cor. ii. 7.
The Revelation of the Mystery	Rom. xvi. 25.
The Mystery of God's Will	Ephes. i. 9.
The Mystery which had been hid in God	Ephes. iii. 9.
The Hidden Wisdom	Ephes. ii. 27.
The Mystery which was kept secret	Rom. xvi. 25.

FIVE LAWS.

The Royal Law	James ii. 8.
The Law of the Spirit of Life	Rom. viii. 2.
The Law ordained by Angels	Gal. iii. 19.
The Law of Liberty	James ii. 12.
The Perfect Law of Liberty	James i. 25.

EIGHT DOCTRINES.

The Doctrine of the Apostles	Acts ii. 42.
The Doctrine according to Godliness	1 Tim. vi. 3.
The Doctrine of Baptisms	Heb. vi. 2.
The Doctrine of Paul	Rom. vi. 17.
The Doctrine of God our Saviour	Tit. ii. 10.
The Sound Doctrine	1 Tim. i. 10.
The Doctrine of Christ	Heb. vi. 1.
The Doctrine of God	1 Tim. vi. 1.

TWENTY-TWO IRREGULAR TITLES.

The Record of the Word of God	Rev. i. 2.
The Message	1 John i. 5.
The Witness of God	1 John v. 9.
The Prophecies which went before on Timothy	1 Tim. i. 18.
The Prophecy of Enoch	Jude 1.
The Epistle of Paul to the Laodiceans	Col. iv. 16.
A more sure Word of Prophecy	2 Pet. i. 19.
The Faith which was once delivered to the Saints *	Jude 3.
The Commandments of the Apostles	2 Pet. iii. 2.
The Scriptures which were able to make Timothy wise unto Salvation	2 Tim. iii. 15.
The Scriptures which John wrote, and which Diotrephes turned out of the Church	Ephes. iii. 9.
The History of the Angels	Jude 6.
The Preaching of Paul	2 Tim. iv. 17.
The Preaching of Jesus	Rom. xvi 25.
The Traditions of the Apostles †	2 Thess. iii. 6.
The Ministry of Reconciliation	2 Cor. v. 18.
The Word of Reconciliation	1 Cor. v. 19.
The Preaching of the Cross	1 Cor. i. 18.
The Foolishness of Preaching	1 Cor. i. 21.
The New Testament †	2 Cor. iii. 6.

---

* *The Traditions of the Apostles* is as evidently the title of a book, or collection of apothegms, as the *New Testament*, and neither phrase could have been used at any time while an apostle was then living — they both belong to the class of modernisms; as also does Jude 3, "The faith which was once delivered unto the saints."

† See note on page 129.

The Foolishness of God . . . . 1 Cor. i. 25.
The Faith of God's Elect . . . . Rom. iii. 3.

It is not contended that all these are titles of books that really existed, though we certainly recognise several of them among the books ascribed to heretics, and several others that are, by the orthodox themselves, admitted to be so; while many more than are thus brought into prominence, might, by a shrewd observance, be culled out from their engagement in the modern fabric, having even more distinct claims than these to be recognised as the pillars of a ruined edifice. Fabricius * informs us that Simon and Cleobius, the most ancient of heretics, had composed books, and given them general circulation, among Christians, under the name of Christ and his Apostles, but we have no account of what they contained or what they were. His authority for this admission is derived from the Apostolic Constitutions, while the probabilities in their favor are infinitely enhanced by the fact that such titles † as they arrogated for those works are really to be found in the epistolary writings of the New Testament, while a name or phrase of any sort that would indicate the Gospel according to Matthew, Mark, Luke or John, is nowhere to be traced.

---

* In Constitutionibus Apostolicis, libro 6, cap. 16, dicuntur Simon et Cleobius hæretici antiquissimi venenatos libros sub Christi nomine composuisse ac vulgasse. Quales vero illi fuerint, vel quid continuerint non constat. — Fabricii, tom. 1, p. 303.

The learned are unanimous in ascribing the Apostolic Constitutions to some impostor, who affixed to them the name of Clemens, Bishop of Rome, in order to procure to them a high degree of authority. — Mosheim.

† Such titles, *e. g.* — The Epistle of Paul to the Laodicians — The Mystery — The Living Gospel — The Treasure of Life.

Every one of the communities addressed in those epistles, whether Romans, Corinthians, Galatians, Ephesians, Philippians, Colossians, or Thessalonians, are addressed as being already Christians, " rooted and grounded in the faith, beloved of God, called of Christ Jesus ; in every thing enriched, in all utterance, and in all knowledge, " &c., &c. The Galatians, in particular, were so certainly possessed of the proper and " genuine gospel," that the Apostle, in the truly apostolic spirit, hesitates not to declare, that if an angel from heaven should preach any other Gospel, he MIGHT BE CURSED. (Gal. i. 8.) Yet nothing is more certain than that, according to the tables of Dr. Lardner, this Epistle was written at least eleven years before any one of our four Gospels; and according to the Epistle itself, the Gospel which the Galatians had received, was not only not the same in substance, but not in the least degree resembling the contents of any one of our Gospels. So that the apostolic curse lights on the believers and preachers of the Gospels that have come down to us.

Nothing, indeed, can exceed the inveteracy of the orthodox against the heretics and their books, and the examples of bitter cursings and revilings which the good shepherds set to the lambs of the Gospel. The Presbyter, Timothy, admonishes his Christian flock that * " those writers, hated by God, had new-fangled to themselves devilish books," (though these happen to be the books, whose titles can be traced in the Epistles of the New Testament, where the orthodox Gospels cannot) and † which

---
* Οι θεοσυγεῖς καινοτομϵσιν εαυτοῖς δαιμονιώδη βιβλια.

† Α συνεταξαν οι αυτοι, θεολντες δόκησιν απ υφηναι την ϛαρκωσιν αυτϵ και ϵ'κ ϵν αληθεία — οτι δε ταῦτα ψευδῆ εισιν' ακϵϛ των αποστολικῶν. Ὁρᾶτε τα ἐπ' ὁνοματι ἱμῶν παρ ασεβῶν κρατυνθεντα βιβλία, μη παραδεχεσθαι. Ου γὰρ τοις ονομάσι χρη υμᾶς προσεχειν των αποστολων ἀλλὰ τῃ φυσει των πραγμάτων, κὰι γνωμη τῃ ἀδιάστροφω.

they wrote themselves, with a design of making it appear that Christ's incarnation had taken place only in a vision, but not in reality; which design as it happens, really does appear in the most general tenor and overt sense of every one of those epistles. But that these are false — " * Hear the Apostolicals, take ye care that ye receive not the books which have, under our name, been established among the ungodly, for you ought not to pay attention to the names of the apostles, but to the nature of the things they treat of, and to the sense, which is not to be set aside."

SECTION XI.

PROOFS THAT NO SUCH PERSON AS JESUS CHRIST EVER EXISTED, AND OF THE IMPOSTURE OF THE GOSPEL HISTORY.

THE Rev. Dr. Smith opens his eleventh section, with a quotation, at length, of the third and fourth propositions of the Manifesto, for which I thank him; and immediately calls those propositions " a mass of impudence and misrepresentation so aggravated, that language has no name to designate it ; " for which I do *not* thank him. But as all this is no answer to the argument indicated in the Manifesto, having had quite enough of what the Doctor

---

* Which Apostolical Constitutions are an authority known and admitted on all hands, to be a forgery.

has to say for the benefit of the Manifesto Writer, let us look to what he offers for the instruction of his readers — "That the miraculous facts recorded in the Gospel history did REALLY OCCUR; and that the occasions of their being wrought were WORTHY of such an interposition of divine omnipotence, has been shown with an abundance of evidence, by numerous and well known authors, to whom access, is easy. Within the narrow limits of these pages it is impossible to do justice to the argument." (p. 43.)

Is it indeed? but could no allowance be made for the difficulty of doing justice to the contrary argument within the limits of one single sentence, on a page that had to exhibit ten times that argument?

But why might not the Doctor just have given the names of a *few* of those numerous and well known authors? for though they may be numerous and well known to him, and herein he shows the greatest proof of his extent of reading and research, to be found in his whole treatise; yet it happens that *I*, and I guess some hundreds who have had as good an education in all other respects as his scurrilous reverence, never heard so much as the name of any one of those authors. It certainly could not have been at any time within the last thousand years, that those authors lived, who were in possession of abundant evidence of what had happened seventeen or eighteen hundred years ago; and what is more, it certainly could not have been on this earth that any authors could have lived, competent to teach us what was WORTHY of divine omnipotence. Those who might *pretend* to do so, may be fit tenants for Bedlam Hospital, or fit hearers of the sanctified impieties of Dr. John Pye Smith. But neither Grotius, Doddridge, Paley, or Lardner, would have been pleased to have such a pretence ascribed to them.

2. His second remark is a recurrence to abuse, without an attempt to refute the propositions.

3. His third is of the same character, except inasmuch as his assertion that "*the pretence of reference to the learned Christian advocates, Mosheim and Jones, is a most infamous piece of forgery,*"—would, *with* the abuse, convey also a most formidable argument, were the assertion not itself a most palpable—*Reverend John Pye Smith, Doctor of Divinity.* The reader has only to turn his eye to the Manifesto, and he will see that under these propositions, no reference at all is made either to Mosheim or Jones.

The *last* reference made to Mosheim, and the only reference made to Jones, is by the letter (*d*) in the *second* proposition, to prove, that there are express admissions of ecclesiastical historians, of their utter inability to show WHEN, or WHERE, or by WHOM, this collection of writings (scil. the New Testament,) was first made. If these admissions shall not be found to be full scope and utmost sense, spirit, letter, effect, and intention—just as I have purported to refer to them—to wit, those admissions purporting to be from Mosheim, even in the first volume of his Ecclesiastical History—Cent. 1, part 2, chap. 2, sect. 16, vol. 1, p. 108. London, 1811, 8vo. edition. And those admissions purporting to be from Jones, even in his work on the Canonical Authority of the New Testament, vol. 1, pp. 2, 4, 23, 41, 173. Then is, Doctor John Pye Smith a scholar, whose learning is respectable, and a gentleman whose word may be depended on; and I, a *guilty forger.* In the other alternative, I shall only claim that the reader will retain the very highest possible respect for Doctor John Pye Smith, that may be compatible with a conviction, that he has said of me the thing that was untrue — that when his charity ran stark staring wild, his veracity ran after it — that he has used abuse instead of argument, and invention instead of truth.

4. His fourth remark, (p. 44,) continued to the end of the section, (p. 53,) presents us with the best piece of writing and of reasoning in his whole essay. Here, for a while, suspending the operation of those malignant and intolerant feelings which, throughout the rest of his composition have so evidently debilitated his understanding, destroyed his respect for truth, and obtunded his perception of reason, — the reader is relieved, by finding that in a lucid interval, the doctor still exhibits the vestiges of mind enough to fill his ministerial and academic avocations, no doubt with sufficient respectability. He can copy the everlastingly bandied passages of Tacitus and Pliny, and string together the thousand times repeated sophisms upon these passages, which thousands have strung together before him. Let him have his due praise, this is really learning at Homerton College. The translations of Tacitus and Pliny — if one were sure that it were the boy's own, is fair enough for a boy of the first form: and as this engagement keeps our author, at least for eight or nine pages, from the use of foul language, it is highly creditable to him.

The argument here assumes a *general* character, and may now be met on fair and general grounds. It shall be so: every concession that historical evidence or even historical probability can challenge, we will yield, grant, offer, not only with willingness, but with alacrity, not only consenting to all such advantages to the Christian argument, as Christians themselves may choose to insist on: but lending the disinterested help of our own historical researches, and throwing over to them whatever *we* may find, and they may have overlooked, that can by any inference seem likely to serve their argument. We wish not an easy victory: the harder they drive on us, the better they please us, and the acrimony of their style, is only grievous to us, because it weakens and breaks off the points of their argument. We serve the cause of truth only; and if truth be not on our side, we wish to surrender, and long to be defeated.

THE TESTIMONY OF TACITUS.

Granted, then, be the genuineness of the passage, so often adduced from the 44th section of the 15th book of the Annals of Tacitus. *Granted*, I pray observe! not because it is wholly incontestible, or that we have not good and tenable ground for a brave conflict against its claims: but, because it is, after all, fully and fairly probable, and *may be*, all and every thing that it purports to be. But what is that purport?

It is the testimony of one of the wisest and best of men that ever lived in all the tide of time — one of the most philosophical lovers of truth — most diligent investigators of the truth he loved, and most faithful historians of the truth he found. He flourished in the beginning of the second century, and it may be admitted wrote this famous passage, about the year which Dr. Lardner assigns to it, A. D. 110. Yet being such a man, and living so near, or as much nearer as you please to the source and fountain-head of all that could be known, or by his diligent inquiry, found out, of Christ, of Christians, and of Christianity; he found no more, and has recorded no more than established his own conviction: and may establish ours, that the Christians were prodigiously wicked men — "HUMANI GENERIS ODIO CONVICTI — PER FLAGITIA INVISI" — "SONTES ET NOVISSIMA EXEMPLA MERITI" and Christianity an "EXITIABILIS SUPERSTITIO" — a damnable superstition. If evidence in favor of a divine revelation ever existed, why was it withheld from Tacitus." If divine inspiration ever guided the pen of man, why was it wanting here?

THE LETTER OF PLINY, (the 97th of his 10th book,) referred to in the index of my Dutch edition—as "Christianorum res in quantum Plinio innotuere." The affairs of Christians, (as far as they were known to Pliny,) of course is of the reign of Trajan, to whom it was written, and is by Dr. Lardner supposed to have been composed, about A. D. 107—it is the only undoubted document of Christianity in the time of that writer. That writer, too, is on all hands admitted to be one of the most wise and virtuous of mankind—a man of whom it would cost us the most laborious effort of imagination to concede that he would for any consideration have dissimulated or suppressed any truth that ever came to his knowledge. He had diligently inquired into what the doctrines of the Christians then were— but what was the result of the inquiry? There was the name indeed of Christ and Christians, but not a precept, not a doctrine, not a circumstance, not an iota of Christianity. "Nihil aliud inveni quam superstitionem pravem et immodicam"—are his words. "*I have found nothing else but a wicked and excessive superstition.*" This is the result of an inquiry into the evidences of the Christian religion, made by the most candid, the most liberal, the most learned, the most virtuous, the most able inquirer, that could be conceived to have existed in all the world, and he, prosecuting that inquiry, seventeen hundred years nearer to the original sources of information than any man now in the world.

If it be objected, that being a Pagan he had less respect for truth, or needed the aid of divine revelation to sooth the asperities of unsanctified nature, to soften his temper, to polish his manners, to control his passions, to give generosity to his sentiments and courtesy to his language; only let the reader compare the style and tone of his epistolary correspondence throughout, with the specimen Dr. John Pye Smith presents of the advantages which Christianity gives to a Doctor of Divinity. In the judgment of Midas, the pipe of Pan was more melodious than Apollo's lute; and an evangelical auditory may perhaps find a style more in harmony with their own feelings in the holy ruffianism of the Christian Priest, than in the scrupulous veracity and tranquil elegance of the Pagan historian.

A Pagan, for instance, (and the Writer of the Manifesto professes no higher character,) would start back, not like the Christian, indeed, with execrations and curses; (for bitter revilings really are curses;) but with surprise at the finesse, the *ruse*, the palpable argumentative swindle, that a man who had ever maintained the divinity of Christ, and taught his congregation "that that mystical being had been born without having a human father; that he raised the dead to life; that he, himself, survived, after having been dead, and in that body which had really died; had visibly ascended in, and through the visible heavens;" should turn round on his choused and cheated hearers, and tell them that the Jews and Heathens, who never once, in any way, nor in the remotest inuendo, had hinted at any one of those events, had told "ALL THE PRIMARY FACTS on which that religion rests."

Good God! and isn't the resurrection of Christ a *primary* fact? Rests not his religion upon that? Can Christianity be true, or true in any part or iota of it, if *that* be false? So judged not the Apostles, when in their first assembly they maintained that the whole sum and effect of the divine commission which they pretended, had constituted them Apostles, for no other purpose than that they should be " witnesses of his resurrection." (Acts i. 22.) So judged not, so argued not the apostolic chief of sinners, in his celebrated 15th to the Corinthians; wherein he makes the resurrection of Christ to be not merely a primary fact, but THE primary fact: and not merely THE primary fact, but the *totum*, the *whole*, the *everything*; the *sine qua non* of Christianity. " If Christ be not risen then is our preaching vain, and your faith is also vain. Yea, and we are found false witnesses of God." (15.) And turns it up at last, that a man will have the impudence to call himself a Christian minister, who maintain that Jews and Pagans have borne witness to all the primary facts; and that if the New Testament and all other Christian writings were blotted out of existence; the writings of decided enemies to the Christian religion, would be sufficient to establish all the primary facts on which that religion rests!

What is *this*, in other words, but to fight desperate for Christianity, to throw it over for dog's meat, and give it up entirely. For who may not be as good a Christian as Dr. Smith, who shall just believe as much of Christianity, and no more, than what Heathens and Jews have recorded? If the Doctor has found any one, Heathen or Jew, who has recorded any one of the primary facts of Christianity, his researches may well be reckoned to put the labors of a Lardner to the blush.

But what should you say, reader, to the logic of a reasoner, who, finding from various " unquestionably authentic writings" of persons who had no *love of the marvellous*, and no intention to countenance or to extend the belief of improbable stories, that there really was, or might have been, such a person as Baron Munchausen; "that he lived," and when his life was arrived at its termination, "he died, at the precise period, which the history (of his wonderful adventures) asserts; finding the extensive prevalency of his *(notions,)* at the time, and in the countries which are stated in his *(wonderful history;)* finding also its reception, by immense multitudes of people, who had the complete means of ascertaining whether the sensible facts on which the *(wonderful)* history was founded, had actually taken place or not," &c., &c. (p. 44); what should you say to the logic, that inferred, that here were all the primary facts, and here the sufficient evidence to establish the most true and wonderful adventures of the renowned Baron Munchausen?

Such is the reasoning that would steal an unintended testimony to falsehood and fable, from the pens of historians and philosophers. Change but the names that may be changed, (without altering the merits of the arguments;) suppose it urged in earnest, and not in banter; and urged with the utmost rancor of malice, the deepest cunning of conscious sophistry; the most reckless disregard of truth, and the foulest virulence of low-bred scurril-*slang;* and 'tis the reasoning of *his reverence*, the evangelical Dr. John Pye Smith.

"5. These memorials of antiquity, (continues our author,) will furnish to the reader ample matter for useful reflection." (p. 50.)

They will, indeed; but not, perhaps, to the conclusion

which the doctor would prescribe. His slander on the characters of those "philosophical, elegant, and self-complacent Romans," is a complete vindication of any other object of his calumnies. If reason, humanity, and justice, were, in his judgment, violated by such men as Pliny and Tacitus, it must be his *good* word and his favorable regard, that can alone prove injurious to the character of any man. Should the present age or any other, but assign to me no worse than the reputation of the most equivocal parts of the characters of Tacitus and Pliny, it should leave me room for more than the whole stock of Christian virtues put together. It would be a blasphemy against moral righteousness to attempt a comparison of the character of the best Christian that ever breathed with that of the Propraetor of Bithynia.

Would the Proprietor of Bithynia, think ye, have dishonored his own conscience, by attempting to prop up the religion of Paganism, with so gross a ruse, as to say, that "immense multitudes had the complete means of ascertaining the fact," (p. 44,) such fact say, as that, of the resurrection of Christ; knowing that no one individual on the face of the earth had any means of ascertaining that fact; and that of that pretended fact, there absolutely was no witness at all?

Would Pliny, think ye, have reasoned with so insolent a contempt of reason, as to ask the question; "If any could have divulged a secret, injurious to the cause would he not have done so!" When he knew that the cause was too contemptible to be injured by any thing; and that, if there were any secret in the business, that secret was always kept from the knowledge of the people, Matt. xiii. 11; Luke viii. 10.

The reader will now see, (immaterial as the question,

whether such a person as Jesus Christ ever existed, in itself may be,) how far from admissions, and much further still from *proofs* of his existence, are what Celsus, Porphyry, Hierocles, Julian, Tacitus, or the Jews, might say about him; and without saying which, they could absolutely not speak of him at all. Shakspeare, we know, speaks of John-a-Dreams. We have all heard of Will-o'-the-Wisp, and Jack-a-lanthorn, Tom-Thumb, and Jack the Giant-killer; and if the day were not too far gone by for histories of these evangelical personages to be foisted in the belief of the people, and *their* belief to be rendered a source of enormous wealth, and the means of measureless extortion to the cunning hierarchy who were really in the guilty secret, and who endeavoured to make it respectable, by associating it with all those moral proprieties which man's nature cannot but love, in whatever associations they are found; so that the people might be brought to believe, that it was Will-o'-the-Wisp had taught them to be just, honest, and sober, to pay their debts, to tell no lies, and to do as they would be done unto: How, I ask, would it be possible for the Celsuses, Porphyrys, and Hierocles, the good and virtuous few, to set about reclaiming the people from so gross a delusion, without soothing and conciliating their attention, by recognizing what was good, and admitting what was probable in their conceit.

As one should say to the fanatic, who would not be civil to one, if one didn't say it, " Ah, well-a-day! be as just, sober, honest, and humane, as Will-o'-the-Wisp has taught you to be; and Will-o'-the-Wisp was, unquestionably, a very good fellow for teaching you so." Would this be admitting his real existence, would this be any proof that the person who so argued, was not aware that

WILL-Ó'-THE-WISP was a phantom; and, like Jesus Christ, had really no prototype in nature, but was merely an *ens* of conceit, a figment of delirium, proceeding from the heat-oppressed brain !

"The poet's eye," says a poet, who dared not have spoken what he meant more plainly,

"In a fine frenzy rolling,
Doth glance from earth to heaven, from heaven to earth.
And as imagination bodies forth
The form of things unknown, the poet's pen
Turns them to shape, and gives to airy nothing
A local habitation and a name."

There is no difficulty, then, in accounting for the wildest romance that ever entered into a romantic brain's invention, coming to quadrate, synchronize, and dovetail into many probable and real circumstances of time and place. Nay, you could not tell a tale if you were to try, without premising or supposing a sort of " *Once upon a time*," or in some such country as had somewhere a real existence, and whose history would furnish the scaffolding for the baseless fabric of your vision. 'Tis hardly more a rule than a necessity of invention laid down by Horace,

"Aut verum aut sibi convenientia finge."

" Either stick to the truth or feign such things as stick together with themselves." The problem then is not how, or wherefore, the hero of a romance should come to be supposed to have lived at such a time and place, or how a thousand co-incident chances, events, and circumstances, which were undeniably true, should happen to concur and fall in with the thread of his fabulous history; especially when all the learning and ingenuity of the world had been for many hundred years employed in seeking for, exaggerating or fabricating such incidental concurrences; but the difficulty is to account for the *how-it-should-have-been*, and wherefore, if the hero in question had a *real* existence, and had been any *such* a personage as he is assumed to be, that we should not have had *more* than evidence of this sort; that philosophers should not have believed, that historians should not have recorded, that the whole world should not have rung with the fame of his exploits; and as the order of nature was suspended to attest his divinity, that the order of nature should not have been suspended to confirm the attestation.

The admissions of the enemies of Christianity would yet have weight with them, if we had but sufficient evidence that those enemies had fair play and were not constrained by the necessity of the times, to temporize and soothe down the ferocious intolerance and sanguinary impatience of Christians, as wise men are sometimes obliged to do congee to madmen; or, if we had not evidence in characters of blood, to the direct contrary. We should in all probability, have never have heard of the objections of Celsus; had Celsus been allowed to go the length he would have done; or had not his writings saved themselves from the flames to which others were consigned, by temporizing and conceding some points, which Origen thought might be turned to good, telling on the Christian side of the argument. And is not Doctor Smith himself conscious of the spirit of Origen's policy? If he can conflict with the arguments here offered to him, he may endure that his congregation should hear of them; but if nothing be conceded, if not an inch of ground be yielded, why of course, and of sound discretion too, he'll do his best, that they shall know nothing about them.

The whole world's history, and that of our own country

most especially, evinces how slowly and gradually even the outworks of Christianity have been yielded — and with what a pertinacious and sanguinary obstinacy, not only the essentials, but the outermost fringes of Christianity, have been maintained. Not two hundred years is it since Dr. Leighton had his nose slit, his ears cut off, and eleven years imprisonment, for only writing a book against the Jure-Divino-ship of Bishops. Not twenty years is it, that Unitarian Christians have been safe from penal statutes; and God have mercy on them yet, if Dr. John Pye Smith's voice or wish could affect the legislation of England. And here am I the tenant of a gaol, at this moment, because my writings have not made concessions enough to Christianity to have been pleaded in mitigation of punishment — because my orations afforded no 'vantage ground to the tact of Christian sophistry.

But as in every individual, and most strikingly perhaps in Dr. John Pye, so in every country we find the greater the prevalence of the Christian religion the more rude the manners, and the more cruel the dispositions of its professors. So we find that it is in the foul-mouthed IRVING's country, and in those *pure* days of genuine religion among his ancestors, which he is ever so delighted to recall; — " In Scotland a greater refinement of cruelty in inflicting torture was adopted than in any other country. *There* the innocent relations of a suspected criminal were tortured in his presence to wring from him, by the sight of *their* sufferings, what no corporal pain inflicted upon himself could extort from him. Thus, in 1596, a woman, being accused of witchcraft, her husband, her son, and a daughter, a child of seven years old, were all tortured in her presence to make *her* confess." — See Arnott's *Crim. Trials*, p. 368, quoted in Aikin's Life of King James the 1st. vol. 2. p. 167.

Pretty fellows, these good Christians, to make us believe that a Divine Revelation has done something for their morals, that a Tacitus or a Pliny could have needed.

6. The ספר תולדות ישו Seper Toldoth Jeschu, which the doctor introduces as his climax of authorities in admission of the real existence of Jesus Christ, and the reality of his miracles, instead of making "*a more than this*," (p. 53.) for his argument really makes less of it. It is an absolute deduction, and throws an air of suspicion over his whole purpose; for how can any admission of the real existence of Christ and of his miracles be inferred or avail, from a palpably furtive document, of which the doctor says that it was written in the middle ages.

"I am of opinion," says the shrewd and cautious Lardner, "that Christianity does not need such a testimony nor such witnesses. It is a modern work, written in the fourteenth or fifteenth century, and is throughout, from the beginning to the end, burlesque and falsehood."— Lardner, vol. 3, p. 574. What a learned wise-acre is the Rev. Dr. Smith, who quotes as his *more than everything else*, and his crowning proof of the real existence of Jesus, the admission of a writer whose admissions were not only not true, but were never written with an intent to pass for truth.

7. And "here, then," concludes the Doctor, "here is a body of evidence, far more than sufficient than to prove that the PERSONS of whom the Scriptures of the New Testament treat, REALLY DID EXIST, and that the *events* which they relate really DID TAKE PLACE (as a consequence, I suppose, of their existence) — " *Give him an inch !*" the proverb is somewhat musty !

But why this "far more than sufficient" in *opem me copia fecit !* Surely *sufficient* would most probably be *sufficient*, but when you give us far more than sufficient, you are palpably *cramming* us.

SECTION XII.

THAT THE GOSPEL NARRATIVES ARE DERIVED FROM THE IDOLATROUS FICTIONS OF INDIA, EGYPT, GREECE, AND ITALY.

HERE the reverend Doctor's Christian indignation loses all bounds — 'tis evident that there is something in the Manifesto that stings him into madness. Its writer, he says, " seems determined to post himself as *the most false of all* that have ever disgraced the use of language." Alas! that the reverend Doctor should seem so determined to dispute that pre-eminence! I believe it would cost a cleverer man than I am, a struggle to win the paragonship of lying from the Professor of Homerton College. For instance were an ordinary hatchet-thrower to do his best in this way, he could only tell his lie off and off, and the first fool he met with would find it out, and there's an end on't; but the Doctor — the Reverend Doctor of Divinity, beats all the Bachelors and Masters of Arts in Europe; and in the very act, and by the very means of making your hair stand at end with horror at the charges he brings against others, is doing it himself all the while: his way being to set Gawkey's mouth open with wonderment at the accusation that he alleges, and then down his throat, in a trice, goes — "*far more than sufficient.*"

For your life, you would have thought that he was honest.

SECTION XIII.

THE INDIAN JESUS CHRIST.

1. "Some, many, or all of these events, (scil. the events related in the New Testament,) had been previously related of the gods and goddesses of Greece and Rome, and more especially of the Indian idol, Chrishna, whose religion, with less alteration than time and translations have made in the Jewish scriptures, may be traced in every dogma, and every ceremony of the evangelical mythology." Such are the words of the fourth proposition of the Manifesto. Now, how are they answered by the Reverend D. D.? Why, in the perfectly evangelical way of doing it. They are at once, without any shadow of attempted disproof, rudely and disgustingly pronounced —" an impudent falsehood!" even in the very sentence which the Doctor has cast on purpose to carry down a falsehood of such transcendent impudence, as nothing but the hurly-burly of ruffianly abuse could have screened from our detection, and sheltered from our scorn.

2. The numerous and well known school-books, entitled Pantheons, Mythological Dictionaries, &c., do not contain refutations, much less ample ones, of the proposition of the Manifesto; nor is it possible that they could have done so, they themselves being of earlier date than the Manifesto. Nor do they affect to refute the sense and purport of the proposition, as it may have been previously maintained by other writers. Nor was it compatible with any purpose of those dictionaries, that they should have done so; nor would they have been admitted into schools,

or have been proper for the use of schools, if they had, as being rendered thereby books of polemical controversy, rather than of classical instruction. Moreover, being generally edited by clergymen, or persons directly concerned and interested in the universal cheat of " training up a child in the way he should go " — they have all of them the most direct and constraining interest to oblige them laboriously and vigilantly to stand off and forbear, even from the outermost purlieus of such a refutation. To have refuted, would have been to have suggested the resemblance. And as the modest asterisks in the Delphin classics, indicating the passages which are too indecent and obscene to be translated, always serve to direct the boy's eye to the very passage which he is sure to understand better than any other part of the book, even because his research is provoked by the effort made to elude it: so an attempt in any way to have shown that there was no resemblance between the Apollo of mythology and the Jesus of the New Testament, the Bacchus and the Moses, would have shown more than the reverend editors could wish to be seen. It was to their purpose to put forth so much of the Pagan mythology as was necessary to enable the stupid lout to make some *hold-together* sense of the text of Pagan authors, but nothing was further from their purpose than to play at asterisks with him on such a delicate subject, or to have startled him into perceptions, suspicions, and investigations, that would have been fatal at once to his loutishness and to his faith.

The Doctor's assertion, then, is not only NOT TRUE, as he knows himself, but not within the measures of a probability of being true, as any body else may know.

3. And to tell his readers, as he does, " that if they

receive the proposition of the Manifesto as true (which really is so) they must have sacrificed reason and conscience to the darkest depravity of soul," (p. 54.) only shows that he must have calculated upon finding readers as patient of being insulted, as they were easy to be deceived. He offers them blustering for their understandings, and defiance for their feelings. His style betrays his habits, his language tanks of his shop. He is used to address a congregation for whom ANY THING will do — a congregation delighted to be deceived, and charmed to be abused. Go it, Doctor! tell 'em, he that believeth not may be damned — tell 'em what "hell-deserving sinners" they are — tell 'em that it's of the Lord's mercy only that they are not consumed — tell 'em that they are all as an unclean thing, and all their righteousness are as filthy rags! Give it 'em — lay it on. In one word, for every thing that is suitable, both for them and you — GOSPEL them. Those who will read both sides of the question, will not endure to be charged with depravity of soul, whatever their decision may be.

4. CHRISHNA. So is spelt the name of the favorite god of the Indian women, in the Manifesto: but *Krishna*, or *Krishnu*, is the way in which the Doctor chooses to spell it; charging the Manifesto Writer with "having altered the spelling of the word, apparently with the base design of giving it a closer resemblance to the sacred name of our Divine Lord." (p. 54.) Oh! for the sacred name of our Divine Lord! But here again, with all this cant, this severe charge of "altering with a base design," is brought against the Writer of the Manifesto, like all the other charges in this scurrilous answer, to cheat and bilk the reader out of the exercise of his impartiality, and to make his own falsehood slip down unperceived in

the torrent of his invective against another. For, all the alteration in the spelling of the name, and consequently all the baseness and design of that altered spelling, happens to be his own. And his apparent design, too apparent, indeed, to be concealed, was, by altering the spelling, which he *has* done, and *I* have *not*, to suppress and keep back from observance, the close resemblance of the names of the idol of the Indian, and the Divine Lord of the European women.

The spelling of the name in the *Asiatic Researches*, by Sir William Jones, (the fountain-head, and first and highest authority, from which I quoted it) will be found to be not *Krishna*, nor *Krishnu*, but as it is exhibited in the Manifesto CHRISHNA. Sir William Jones is, on all hands, admitted to be the most competently informed and most learned investigator of this recondite subject; and in addition to his being on all hands admitted to be one of the most accomplished philologers and prodigies of intellectual acquirements that ever breathed, if not the *facile princeps* of the whole world in these respects; *he* was also a sincere and ardent Christian. He expressly avows and maintains his conviction as a Christian, in so many words — " the adamantine pillars of our faith cannot be shaken by any investigation of Heathen Mythology." And in another passage — " I, who *cannot help* believing the divinity of the Messiah, from the undisputed antiquity and manifest completion of many prophecies, &c., am obliged, *of course*, to believe the sanctity of the venerable books to which that SACRED PERSON refers." — Vol. I, p. 233.

Yet the words of Sir William Jones, this unquestionably first, highest, and best authority on the subject are — and I pray the reader's observance, that I give even his spelling of the words : —

"That the name of CRISHNA, and the general outline of his story, were long anterior to the birth of our Saviour, and probably to the time of Homer, we *know very certainly*."— Asiatic Researches, Vol. I, p. 259. I ask the reader, then, to direct his researches to those researches! I ask the Christian to say whether he can suspect that this Christian writer would have spelt the name CRISHNA rather than Krishna, or Krishn*u*, with a base design of producing an apparent resemblance where there was none in reality? I ask his candor to decide whether this unquestionably sincere Christian would have spelt the name as he has done without the most constraining evidence to determine his mind, that *that* was the essentially correct spelling? and whether after his long residence in India, and laborious studies into the Asiatic Mythologies, he would have spoken so positively without having grounds and reasons for doing so that are not to be yielded to the arbitrary conjectures or impudent denials of subsequent critics, of interested, crafty quibblers, who want to get out of it now at any rate, and who, smarting under the irresistible inferences which we have drawn, wish their own man at the devil for having given us such good ground for our inferences? and *now* forsooth, that the spell tells against them, they won't give their prodigy of learning credit for knowing how to spell. Mr. Beard, the Unitarian opponent of my forty-fourth oration, in which I first put forth this important argument, had consulted the authority. HE presumed not to deny that the original name of the Indian idol was indeed spelt CRISHNA, but denies the resemblance. It was too bold a stroke, with the text of Sir William Jones before him, to let down his sledge hammer upon CRISHNA — so he claps the Latin termination US, to CHRIST, making it CHRISTUS, and thus gets a syllable further off from the suspicious resemblance. "In the names CHRISHNA and CHRISTUS, there are four letters similar, and six dissimilar," says he, "and therefore the two words are not identical." See his 3d Letter to the Rev. Robert Taylor, p. 85. Reader! see what Latin can do! though by the bye it seems to spoil a man's arithmetic. Six and four used to be ten, but an' if a man had not more learning than wit, he could count but eight in *Christus*, even with its Latin termination. But, take away the Asiatic termination *na* from Chrishna, and let *Christ* stand in plain English, and Chrish and Christ are like enough to pass, the one for the ghost of the other. But, Oh no! is the cry-out of the Evangelical mystics, "Take any shape but that, and my firm nerves should never tremble."

"5. From a few and distant resemblances," says our author, "in the midst of a chaos of acts and qualities, the most opposite, it would be highly unreasonable to draw the conclusion that there was any real conformity in history or character."

This is admitting something. The Rev. Mr. Beard, an infinitely more formidable opponent, and it would be no compliment to any man to say a more respectable one than Dr. Smith admits the resemblance of four good points out of the round dozen for which I had, in my Clerical Review — a work which I published in Ireland — stoutly contended. He admits that

I. Chrishna was in danger of being put to death in his infancy, a tyrant, at the time of his birth, having ordered all new-born males to be slain.

II. Chrishna performed miracles.

III. Chrishna preached.

IV. Chrishna washes the feet of the Brahmins.

Now the reader has only to recollect the fable of the Lion and the Statuary, and its moral will admonish him, that as the man would certainly not have been uppermost, if the beast had been the carver; so in this exhibition of the rival claims of Christ and Chrishna, he is to be on the *qui vive*, for the opposite motives and interests of the opposing parties, and so make the corresponding deductions for the colorings they will severally lay on their respective pictures, according as they wish to conceal or to expose the resemblance in question. Not only will the Christian artists lay on the vermilion upon the cheek of their God, but they'll lose no sly opportunity of throwing me over a patch of lamp-black upon mine. I shall have hard work to get an eye for an eye, and a tooth for a tooth from them: the very same line which they shall say is *crooked* upon my canvass, shall pass for straight on theirs. *Exempli gratia* — Does my Chrish wash the feet of the Brahmins his disciples? — Why to be sure it was an obscene, disgraceful, and contemptible action, and none but a slave or a fool would have done it, and I cannot deny it. But, catch we their Chrish in the self same act, — Oh, then it was infinite condescension and divine humility.

Does my Chrish spend a little of his leisure time with the milk-maids and rustic damsels in dancing, sporting, and playing on the flute? Why the very worst construction is put on it, and they declare that, notwithstanding his own preaching to the contrary, he exhibited an appearance of excessive libertinism.

But *their* Chrish may have his sweethearts, Mary and Martha: his Magdalene, (none of the most reserved of ladies,) his Joan and Susan,* and many others, who whatever other attentions they have paid him, " did also minister to him of their substance!" and scandal must not hint what it must n't hint. — Luke viii. 3.

Does *my* Chrish breathe a vein occasionally, or cut a throat or two, and encourage his disciples to do the like? why 'twas bad enough, and God knows he was a scoundrel for doing so.

But does *their* Chrish order his ." enemies that would not have him to reign over them to be brought forth and slain before him!" (Luke xix. 27.) Why, that you know was only in the figurative language of a parable.

Does he give it in charge to his disciples that — "if any of them had not a sword he should sell his garment and buy one." (Luke xxii. 36.) Why those swords, you know, were not meant to commit murder with.

Has the prevalence of his religion in all countries and ages of the world, proved to be the greatest curse that ever befell the human race? And are the banners and trophies of bloody massacres and wholesale villanies, the worst and most horrible that imagination could conceive, still hanging, still to be seen among the ornaments of the most magnificent temples consecrated to his grim-Godhead? Why you must call him the Prince of Peace and the Lamb of God; and his religion must be considered as the source of civilization, morals, and virtue among men; and should an honest man venture to speak his

---

* Nobody knows much about this Susan, but Joan was certainly another man's wife. A good example this, for our itinerant preachers to set before the ladies of their congregation, to rob their husbands to support a reformer; ? wouldn't it have been more honourable of Jesus, to have made a few loaves and fishes for his own use?

mind freely, or say but half of what *they* would say of Chrishna, if they had but half as much reason for saying it: it isn't long ago since they'd have killed him on the spot. It is mercy, and humanity, and all that sort of stuff, that has let me off with my life, and only deprived me of my liberty, for laughing where I could not help laughing, and throwing out a hint that in *my* conceit it is not " WORTHY of an interposition of divine omnipotence." p. 43. to steal asses, to destroy young trees, to upset market-stalls, and to persecute pigs: and that if the Son of God had a mind to show off his heir apparentship, he shouldn't have exhibited in the most obscure and contemptible village in all his father's dominions, among the very scum and scamps of the whole human race, where indeed he was not likely to meet with better treatment than that, which I suppose has cured him of keeping low company, (93d Oration.)

" In the Sanscrit Dictionary, compiled more than two thousand years ago, (says Sir William Jones,) we have the whole story of the incarnate Deity born of a virgin, and miraculously escaping in his infancy from the reigning tyrant of his country," &c. See his Asiatic Researches, Vol. I. pp. 259, 260, 267, 272, 273. And for further coincidences in the two fabulous histories of the two fabu-deities, call in the illustrations to be derived from the Apocryphal Gospels, in which it will be found that those earlier narratives retained features of coincidence, which, since the art of gospelling has been better understood, have been *judiciously* pruned away.

The Unitarian editors of the New Testament, strain every nerve to get the whole account of Herod seeking the young child to destroy him, and slaying all the children that were in Bethlehem, and in all the coasts thereof, from two years old and under, Matt. ii. 16, whom " God made to glorify him by their deaths," *(Church of England Collect,)* ejected from the canonical scriptures. It betrays two much of its real origin. And if the art of printing, and the vigilant observance of infidels, did not make Christians stick to their text, even when it gravels them, this pretty story would be apocryphized, and in a few years, the possibility of tracing its Indian origin would be lost.

But observe now, the retrogressive stages of imposture. When grosser materials and huger absurdities, suited the brute appetite of miracles and wonderment, that ever characterizes ignorant minds, the Apocryphal Gospels, the Gospels as they were, did well enough: when awakening intelligence, or exhausted gullibility, called for something more within the limits of a *conceivable* possibility; universal acquiescence, hailed the *improved Version*, and the Gospels as revised, castigated, and accommodated to the improved notions and better information of mankind, *according* to the learned Bishops, Matthew, Mark, Luke, and John; who, (whoever they were,) would long retain the gratitude of Christians, and be considered as the very highest authority for the able and judicious abridgements they had made.

Increasing shrewdness, however, calls again for a revision of the evangelical compilations; *more* pruning and cutting-off is needed. What served for the dolts and savages some hundred years ago, will serve no longer. The Unitarian editors offer themselves to do for a more enlightened age, what the Anti-Nicene Bishops had done for earlier times. Subsequent editors will Unitarianize upon Unitarianism itself, and the Gospel according to Richard—and the Gospel according to Robert, shall beat even the Unitarian Version into acknowledged apocrypha.*

EXAMPLE 1. In the great prototype and earliest pattern of gospel making, we read, that Chrishna when an infant, was accused by certain nymphs of having drank their curds and milk, his mother reproves him for this act of theft, which he stoutly denied, and in vindication of his innocence requested her to examine his mouth — when, behold, she beheld the whole universe, in all its plenitude and magnificence.—Vol. 1. Asiatic Researches. Well, such a story was out-Heroding Herod, and, therefore, must be *apocryphized* ; but 'twas a pity to lose the conceit entirely; you shall find it in another shape, in the *canonical* Gospel of Matthew, chap. iv. 8. where the Devil taketh Christ up into an exceeding high mountain, and showeth him all the kingdoms of the world, and the glory of them. Here the judicious *Bishop* Matthew, by bringing in the condition, that the mountain was *exceeding high*, forestalls any objection to the improbability of the story, since it could be easily *demonstrated*, that, if the mountain was high *enough*, any body might see far enough; and though " the whole universe in all its plenitude and magnificence," must have been rather too large a mouthful for a little boy; yet, by the help of the devil, a man's eye might be brought to take in an exceeding wide range of prospect. Here, you see, is evident *new working* upon an old material, the ground is the same, the building re-constructed.

EXAMPLE 2. In the original history of Chrishna, we read, that he held up a mountain on the tip of his little finger — well! this would not do for the Western world;

---

* The fact as stated in the Manifesto, really solves the phenomena : Our received Gospels were never offered to the world as originals, their authors never pretended that they were any thing more than compilers of previously existing histories.

but the hint would do to supply the modern Jesus with a good metaphor, when increasing credulity would take it for nothing better. So he tells *his* Brahmins that if they had faith as a grain of mustard-seed, they should remove a mountain, Matt. xxi. 21; and certain 'tis, that the good Bishop, who compiled the story, was aware, that in the way of believing, a great deal could be be removed.

EXAMPLE 3. " And when Jesus went in, the standards bowed themselves and worshipped him."* So ran the original text of the Gospel, from which Luke has introduced his account of the two thieves; of the Gospel, from which alone, the Apostles' Creed introduces the article, " He descended into hell," and, which is evidently referred to, in I Peter iv. 6. But this was become too gross; it was overdoing it. Avast! cries Bishop John, they won't stand that, but let us keep the pith of the story, let us have it, that the *men* who *held* the standards bowed down; so the castigated text became, " As soon, then, as he had said unto them, I am he, they went backward and fell to the ground, John xvi. 6. Which is still a miracle, but not quite such an overfling at it.

Our conquest then, (and in the struggle to conquer so much, I have taken much harder words, than arguments, from my opponents,) amounts to this:†

---

* Nicodemi Evangelium in Fabricii Codice Apocrypho, tom. 1. p. 241.

† 1."Very respectable natives have assured me, that one or two Missionaries have been absurd enough, in their zeal for the conversion of the Gentiles, to urge that the Hindus, were even now almost Christians, because their Brahma, Vishnou, and Mahesa, were no other than the Christian Trinity."— Asiatic Researches, vol. 1. p. 272.

2. " I am persuaded, that a connection existed between the old idolatrous nations of Egypt, India, Greece, and Italy, long before the birth of Moses." — Ibid. p. 271.

1. My Chrishna is the elder, and the first-born, and

2. That by a certainty " long anterior," probably more than nine hundred years priority to their Christ, and

3. That upon the positive knowledge, the " *We know very certainly,* " of Sir William Jones.

4. THAT, their own very highest authority.

---

3. " The second great divinity, Chrishna, the incarnate Deity of the Sanscrit romance, was cradled, as it informs us, among herdsmen; a tyrant at the time of his birth, ordered all new-born males to be slain."—Ibid. p. 259.

4. " His birth, was concealed through fear of the tyrant Cansa, to whom it had been *predicted*, that one born at that time, in that family, would destroy him."—Ibid. p. 259.

5. " He was born from the left intercostal rib of a Virgin, of the royal line of Devaci, and after his manifestation on earth, returned again to his heavenly seat in Vaicontha."—Ibid.

6. " He was fostered, therefore, in Mat'hura, by an honest herdsman, surnamed *Ananda*, or Happy, and his amiable wife Yasoda. The sect of the Hindus, who adore him with an enthusiastic, and almost exclusive devotion—maintain, that CHRISHNA was superior to all the prophets, who had only a portion of his divinity, whereas, Chrishna, was the person of Vishnou himself, in a human form."—Ibid. p 260.

For in him dwelleth all the fulness of the Godhead, bodily.—2 Colossians, 9.

7. " At the age of seven years, he held up a mountain on the top of his little finger."—Asiatic Researches, Vol. 1. p. 273.

8. " He slew the terrible serpent Caliya."

9. " He passed a life of a most extraordinary and incomprehensible nature."—Ibid. p. 259.

10. " He saved multitudes, partly by his arms, and partly by his miraculous powers."

11. " He raised the dead, by descending for that purpose to the lowest regions."

12. " He was the meekest and best tempered of beings, yet he fomented, and conducted a terrible war."

13. " He was pure and chaste in *reality*, but exhibited an appearance of excessive libertinism."—Ibid. Chap. 9.

VINDICATION OF THE MANIFESTO. 151

5. THAT an authority, against which they can with no modesty attempt to pit a counter authority—and

6. THAT an authority, avowedly hostile to our inferences.

7. And CHRISHNA, not Krishna or Krishnu, is his name.

8. And He was a God incarnate.

9. And He was by his human mother descended from a royal race.

10. And He it was, whom the tyrant of his country sought to kill in his infancy.

11. And He it was, on whose account, the tyrant slew all the children, " that glorified God by their deaths."

12. And He it was, who slew a terrible serpent, " *bruised the serpent's head.*"

13. And He it was, who was miraculously born.

14. And He it was, whose whole life was spent in working miracles.

15. And in preaching mysteries.

16. And in washing other people's feet.

17. And He it was, who descended into hell.

18. And He it was, who rose again from the dead.

19. And He it was, who ascended into Heaven, after his death.

20. And He it was, who left his doctrines to be preached by his disciples, but committed nothing of his own to writing.

21. And He it was, who had been the object of prophecy.

Here is "*the general outline,*" and broad facts of a religious romance or SPELL, which, relating the life and adventures of a God manifest in the flesh, would naturally be called a *Spell of God* or a *God's Spell* or a Gospel, admitted to have formed the substance of the secret mysteries of the Brahmin " long anterior to the birth of our Saviour, and probably long anterior to the time of Homer, which was nine hundred years anterior to *that* time." Now reader " search the Scriptures" produce but one text out of the fourteen Epistles of Paul, that seems to speak of the events of the Evangelical narrative, as being then recent, against the twenty, the fifty, or the hundred, which refer to the whole gospel scheme, as being in *his* day altogether of a remote antiquity, which in short are perfectly compatible and entirely congruous with an understanding that it was this general outline of Chrishna and the Hindoo-mythology that he was endeavoring to modernize, and I will yield thee thy more than twentieth part of the probabilities on the opposite supposition.

Why should it have been, that when the Apostolic Chief of Sinners made the best of his Christian tale at Athens, the Philosophers, Epicureans, and Stoics should have been disgusted at him, because, while he was attempting to impose that Therapeutan * romance, on the ignorant and foolish part of the community, he brought to *their* knowledge NO NEW THING. (Acts xvii.) †

Why should he have played off his villainous, wheedling artifices upon the illiterate and ignorant rabble, telling them that *they* were especial favorites of God; that the greater fools, dunces and idiots that they were, the fitter vessels of divine election : that God had chosen

---

* The *Therapeutæ* were an ancient Jewish sect of itinerant quack doctors who professed the art of healing : from whence their name is derived : they were mighty travellers, dealt in charms and spells : and from their plagiarsm, the *Indian* Chrishna, got at last, his *Jewish* physiognomy.

† Paul of Tarsus is unquestionably a real character, and much of his actual history has been tacked on to the fabulous Acts of the Apostles.

the foolish things, the weak things and the base things—
(1 Corinth. 1.) to be rich in faith, that is, to be as they
were likely to be, *the most easily imposed on.*

Why should he have made it a matter of high crime
against the Greeks, that they *sought after wisdom,* that is, in
other words, they wanted something like rational evidence,
proof, argument, or grounds of common sense and rational
probability for his matter? But, he had nothing of that
sort to give them, it was too far off, it was too long ago:
he could give no clue, produce no document, make no
reference, put them into no train of inquiry; not a vistage,
not an iota : not a glimpse or a shadow of any one, even
the most broad and necessary fact that must have existed,
and must have been at that time in hand to have produced,
if such a person as Jesus had existed in any shape whatever. Only they were to believe! Children and fools
may do so! was probably the sentiment of the philosophers—" but, Sir, it is too much to call upon our assent,
to the most stupendous events that imagination could
conceive, upon, absolutely, no *evidence at all!"* This
was the real condition of the argument, when Mr. Beard
would persuade us, that the historical evidences of Christianity were unassailable; while the Apostle, forlorn of
all evidence, desperate of all argument; with an impiety
desperate as his case—and forlorn as his hopes, ascribed
the whole Gospel dispensation, to its origination in the
FOOLISHNESS OF GOD.—1 Corinth. i. 25.

It is admitted, that of Chrishna's history, we have only
the outlines.* But had we the fillings-up, a still closer
resemblance might be traced. What might be wanting

---

* 14. " He washed the feet of the Brahmins, and preached very
nobly indeed, and sublimely, but always in their favor." Sir
William Jones in Asiatic Researches, Vol. 1. Chap. 9.

in the Indian mythology, is abundantly to be supplied, from the idolatrous mythology of Phenician, Druidical, Greek, and Roman superstition.

It is impossible, that within the compass of these pages, I should trust myself in an expatiation on this subject, to which I have for many years devoted my studies, and intend, should my prison hours be extended, to revise and enlarge the works I have already produced.

The ADONIS of the Phenicians, is an undeniable Jesus Christ.—See Parkhurst's Hebrew Lexicon.

The EASTRE from which our English word Easter, is derived, is the Druidical type of Jesus.

The PROMETHEUS of the Greeks, is the crucified God.

The MERCURY, the Word or Messenger of the Covenant is the same visionary conceit.

The APOLLO.

The BACCHUS, and all the idolatrous family, are but the varied embodyings of the same parent, and universally diffused hallucination.

SECTION XIV.

THE EGYPTIAN JESUS CHRIST.

IN the hieroglyphical representations, on the Pyramids of Egypt, Plato, * 348 years before the Christian era,

---

* PLATO *Broadshoulders* died 348 before our Epocha. The beginning of John's Gospel is evidently Platonic. This philosopher was himself believed to have been born of a pure virgin ; and in his writings had drawn up the imaginary character of a DIVINE MAN,

traced the significant symbols of a religion, which the priests informed him, had then existed upwards of ten thousand years. The cross with the man upon it, was the object of Pagan worship, and the significant emblem of the doctrines of the Pagan faith, for countless ages; ere that faith took up its Jewish features, and Minutius Felix, one of the earliest Fathers, taunts them for their adoration of that symbol.* I myself have seen, and many gentlemen at this day possess, lamps brought from the bases of the pyramids of an antiquity, that makes a yesterday of the era of Augustus, and yet shaped so as to present the light that issued from them, before the symbols of the Cross, Eternity, and the Trinity. Nay, the religious honors paid to the NILE, from the time when the ourang-outang ancestors of mankind became sensible of the benefit of its inundations, were necessarily addressed to the upright post with a transverse beam, indicating the height to which its waters would reach, and the extent to which they would carry the blessings of fertilization. The demon of famine was happily expressed, by the naked and emaciated being, nailed upon it: the reed in his hand was gathered from the marshy margin of the river: the NILE

---

whose ideal picture he completed by the supposition that such a man would be CRUCIFIED:

" *Virtue* confessed in human shape he draws,
What Plato *thought*, and GODLIKE Cato was."

See Madame Dacier's Trans. and Clarke's Evidences.

* " You it is ye Pagans who worship wooden Gods, that are the most likely people to adore wooden crosses. Your victorious trophies not only represent a simple cross, but a cross with a man upon it; and whereas ye tax our religion with the worship of a criminal and his cross; you are strangely out of the way of truth to imagine either that a criminal can deserve to be taken for a Deity, or that a mere man can possibly be a God." p. 134, Reeve's Translation.

had smote him with that reed. His crown of thorns emblemized the sterility of the provinces over which he reigned, and his infamous title indicated that he was the king of vagrants and beggars. — *Meagher on the Popish Mass.*

SECTION XV.

THE PHŒCIAN JESUS CHRIST.

A very learned sect or party among divines and critics maintain that the Hebrew points ordinarily annexed to the consonants of the word יהוה Jehovah, are not the natural points belonging to that word, nor express the true pronunciation of it, but are the vowel points belonging to the words Adonai and Elohim, applied to the consonants of the ineffable name Jehovah, to warn the readers that instead of the word Jehovah, the pronunciation of which is now entirely lost, they were to say ADONAI. I have sifted this matter out, by inquiring among the Rabbis and more intelligent Jews, and find, that without any other reason but their religion, they invariably pronounce their mystical tetragrammaton, which we see inscribed even over our Christian altars, A DON : GNAW : YE! as a Scotchman would say "I don't know ye." The word literally signifies, OUR LORD. It is the real ADONIS of the Phœnicians, and the Jesus Christ of those who ought to know better. Not only the names, but the attributes, the legendary history, and the religious rites of these mystical hypostases are the same. Under the designation of TAMMUZ, and as a personification of the SUN, this idol

was worshipped, and had his altar even in the temple of the Lord which was at Jerusalem. Several of the Psalms of David were parts of the liturgical service employed in his worship, the 110th in particular — tho' utterly without any meaning, as gabbled over in our Church service — is an account of a friendly alliance between the two idols יהוה: and אדני: Jehovah and Adonis, in which Jehovah adorns Adonis for his priest as sitting at his right hand, and promises to fight for him against his enemies, and to break their skulls for them. This idol was worshipped at Byblis in Phœnicia, with precisely the same ceremonies: the same articles of faith as to his mystical incarnation, his precious death and burial, and his glorious resurrection and ascension, and even in the very same words of religious adoration and homage which are now, with the slightest degree of newfangledness that could well be conceived addressed to the idol of the Gospel. On a certain night during the passion week, an image representing the suffering God was laid upon a bed; excessive wailings and lamentations constituted an essential part of the mystical solemnities. The attachment of the women to the beautiful deity provoked the jealous Jehovah: and in Ezekiel, chap. vii. verse 14, we find that this mode of idolatry was denounced as a most wicked abomination —
" He brought me to the door of the gate of the Lord's house, and behold, there sat women weeping for Tammuz."
After the lamentations had continued to exhaustion, lights*
were brought in, the image was lifted up from its shrine, and the priests anointed the lips of the assistants in those

---

* Hence those expressions in the idolatrous Psalmography of the Sidonians and Phœnicans—" There is sprung a light for the righteous, and joyful gladness for such as are true-hearted." " Full of grace are thy lips, because God hath anointed thee."

holy mysteries. It was announced that the God had risen from the dead, and the priest addressed the admiring and grateful worshippers in words whose exact sense is retained in our Easter hymn:

"But the pains which he endured,
Our salvation have procured."

In sober prose—Trust ye in God, for out of his pains we receive salvation,*— See Parkhurst's Hebrew Lexicon.

SECTION XVI.

THE ATHENIAN JESUS CHRIST.

† The *Prometheus Bound*, of Æschylus, was acted as a

---

* Θαρειτε τω Θεω εστι γαρ ημιν εκ πονων Σωτηρια.

† My very able and respected opponent the Rev. Mr. Beard, of Manchester, labours as hard to defeat this resemblance of the Grecian tragedy to the Christian romance, as I confess I have done to establish it. But as I labour only for truth, and have no right to impute any other aim to him, I am sorry when I find him condescending to take an advantage in the argument unworthy of his great powers and highly cultivated intelligence. He defies me to point out a line in the tragedy, in which the God Oceanus is called *Petreus*, (p. 52.) I had never implied that there was such a line; but any good classical dictionary would have borne out the strict and literal truth of what I both said and meant—" *Oceanus*, one of whose names was *Petreus*." The conduct of this personage in the process of the drama, is in as close resemblance to that of a fisherman of Galilee as his name Petreus is to Peter. He forsook his friend, when the wrath of God had made him a victim for the sins of the human race. The difference between being crucified on a beam of timber, and nailed exactly in the same manner upon a rock, is not enough to redeem the palpable plagiarism. Let Mr. Beard, however, in welcome, deny all those points of coincidence that I have maintained: his own admissions, when he admits the

tragedy in Athens, 500 years before the Christian era. The plot or fable of the drama, being then confessedly derived from the universally recognized type of an infinitely remote antiquity; yet presenting not one or two, but innumerable coincidences with the Christian tragedy; not only the more prominent situations, but the very sentiments, and often the words of the two heroes are precisely the same. So that there can be no doubt, that as the original was unquestionably a poetical figment, the version was of the same imaginary creation. It has only been since ignorance has happily given way to the inroads of science and philosophy, and men have found the pleasure

---

least, will, I say not to every impartial mind, but surely to every excursive imagination, vindicate the Athenians, for rejecting the doctrine of the Apostle Paul, as being no new thing *to them*. Prometheus made the first man and woman out of clay. Prometheus was a God. Prometheus exposed himself to the wrath of God, incurred by him in his zeal to save mankind. Prometheus, in the agonies of crucifixion exclaimed—

> "See what, a God, I suffer from the Gods;
> For mercy to mankind, I am not deemed
> Worthy of mercy — but in this uncouth
> Appointment am fixed here,
> A spectacle dishonourable to Jove.
> On the throne of Heaven scarce was he seated,
> On the powers of Heaven
> He showered his various benefits, thereby
> Confirming his sovereignty: But for unhappy mortals
> Had no regard, but all the present race
> Willed to extirpate and to form a new:
> None, save myself, opposed his will. I dared,
> And boldly pleading saved them from destruction,
> Saved them from sinking to the realms of night:
> For which offence I bow beneath these pains,
> Dreadful to suffer, piteous to behold!"
>
> Potter's Translation, quoted from memory.

of being rational, that the priests have found it necessary to pretend the existence of a real personage, and a substantial substratum for their system. In the pure primitive days, it wasn't wanted, there was no call for evidence; but now, must the priests go to work, the people want to believe, and to have a reason for it too! and *some* time, *some* place, some probabilities must be invented for them. Well. What was to be done? Why! "Get as far out of sight — and as long ago with your story, as they will patiently endure — say it was in Judea: they had no historians there — say it was in the light of the Augustan era, when every body might have seen all about it: for eleven or twelve hundred years of dark ages have transpired since then; and we're all safe, for now the candle has gone out." Such is the history of Christianity.

The close resemblances, the almost exact conformities of the Christian and Pagan mythologies, were so far from shaking the faith of the first Fathers of the Church, that in a sense perhaps which I shall not be allowed to put on the words of Sir William Jones, they also would have said — " the adamantine pillars of our faith cannot be shaken by any investigation of Heathen mythology." Certainly not! for it was the Heathen mythology itself, that constituted the pillars of that faith; and the resemblance of the one to the other was urged by the first preachers, as their most powerful argument to recommend Christianity, and to induce the Pagans to be converted, seeing that the transition was almost imperceptible, the difference was so very immaterial. Paganism and Christianity were as like as two peas to each other—and in fact, the better and shrewder sort of Pagans, had been Chistians without knowing it.

To one passage only in the Doctor's Treatise will I turn

back, as leading most naturally to the conclusion of this whole argument. I follow a rambling writer, and must be excused for fetching him up to the arrangement he ought to have observed. His objection to the very last position of the Manifesto, occurs 16 or 17 pages before his objections to subsequent positions :—I take him *here*, then —

" It is a perfect insult to common sense, that this man pretends to adduce scripture evidence, that the blessed Jesus never existed." (I pass over his ruffian scurrility) and he adds — " a mere child who can read the New Testament might easily confute," &c. Now this was as easily said, as was the egregious untruth that follows it. But easy, as he may choose to say, it would be to a child to confute that conclusion, he himself is not man enough to do it : and I'll undertake to write myself by any one of the vile opprobious epithets which he has applied to me, if he can find any other child to help him to do it, e'en an' let it be forty or fifty years since that child cut his teeth.

Observe but the canon of critical evidence, which the conviction of all men places on the same basis of certainty as the theorems of the multiplication table — to wit,

AN ABSTRACTION OR PHANTASY OF THE IMAGINATION, MAY BE SPOKEN OF IN TERMS STRICTLY AND LITERALLY APPLICABLE ONLY TO A SUBSTANTIAL AND CORPOREAL BEING — BUT A SUBSTANTIAL AND CORPOREAL BEING, CANNOT HAVE ONE SINGLE ATTRIBUTE PREDICATED OF IT THAT WOULD EXCLUDE THE NOTION OF CORPOREITY, AND BELONG ONLY TO AN ABSTRACTION. You may draw out an allegory to any extent of invention. You may say for instance that " Wisdom dwelt with the sons of men, that she lifted up her voice in the streets, and that she said — whatever any wise or foolish person might say for her;" yet none of these predictions would imply that wisdom was a real and corporeal existence. But say only but *once* in the course of the longest history — that its hero " vanished away " — that he walked on water, rode in the air, or that he appeared alive after being once dead, and we perceive at once, that it *is* an abstraction that has been set before us; and 'tis not the author's dissimulation, but our own stupidity, if we take *that* to be a reality which he gives so sufficient a clue to show us, was nothing more than a figment.

I have on my table the beautiful poem of QUEEN MAB. She rides, she alights from her chariot, she walks, she waves her wand, she speaks, and certainly never spake human being to better effect of excellent good sense, exalted knowledge, and consummate virtue. Was it necessary for its author to warn his readers in so many words, that Queen Mab was only a poetical ecstasy, that no such person as Queen Mab ever had any real existence? Was it not enough to connect her history with circumstances incompatible with the laws of animal existence? THAT, Bysshe Shelley has done for the Fairy — that, the evangelical poetasters have done for the less pleasing demon of the Gospel.

Some of the passages in which they have done so, out of very many to the like effect, are specified in the Manifesto. But "these passages," themselves, says the learned Answerer, "demonstrates the unspeakable folly and wickedness of my mind." How so? or why should the Doctor have said so, if there had been nothing in those passages, that he could wish had not been there? See reader! your Dissenterian priest is as unwilling, that you should have your *own use* of the Scriptures, as ever was the Jesuit or the Pope. The only difference between the two intolerants, is, that the one kept the stable-door locked, and there was no horse to be ridden; the other indeed, lets you have the horse, but only upon condition that you shall ride after his fashion, sit with your face to the crupper, and travel to no other conclusions than he prescribes for you.

The passages referred to in the Manifesto, are

Luke ix. 29.—And as he prayed, the fashion of his countenance was altered, &c.

Mark ix. 2.—He was transfigured, (the Greek signifies *metamorphosed*, entirely and wholly changed, and his apparel is described as undergoing the same metamorphosis.) " And his raiment became shining, exceeding white as snow, so as no fuller on earth can white them."

Luke xxiv. 31.—And their eyes were opened, and they knew him, and he vanished out of their sight.

I John v. 6.—This is he that came by water and blood.

His habiliaments seemed to have shared in his various metamorphoses, to have travelled with him, or to have grown upon him. For, as he certainly left his night-shirt in the sepulchre, when he afterwards appeared in the costume of a gardener to Mary Magdalene; and, no doubt in a decent and becoming manner, to the eleven disciples: unless he had waited on his tailor first, to suit him for such an appearance; a thought, which it is impiety to think, he must have possessed the faculty of producing his own clothing, or have been supplied by fairies and genii. All of which circumstances, his miracles, his miraculous birth, his resurrection after death, his visible ascent into Heaven, the various and contradictory manner of telling the story by the different Evangelists, &c., &c., are incompatible, not only with any idea of his existence as a man, but with any just grounds for accusing the Bishops who compiled the story, of having expected that any rational being would ever come to think that they had intended to represent him as a man.

The reader has only to bear in mind, the certain and unquestionable priority of the Apocryphal Gospels, and the universally admitted superiority, both in intelligence and virtue, of those parties in the early Church, who, not having been so violent and sanguinary as the orthodox, or not so fortunate, were put undermost, and made the *Dissenters* of their day; and, therefore, and only therefore, were called Heretics; and then, he will see the convincing light of evidence from their writings, flash on those that have come down to us—bringing up the dark points, and throwing the unaccountable lines into order, method, and purpose.

SECTION XVII.

HISTORIES OF THE DEMON JESUS, ANTECEDENT TO THE RECEIVED GOSPELS.

1. "WITHIN the immediate year of the pretended crucifixion of Christ, (I cannot bring myself to use the stronger expressions of Gibbon,) sooner than any other account of the matter could have been made known, it was publicly taught, that, instead of having been miraculously born, and having passed through the impotence of infancy, boyhood, and adolescence, he had descended on the banks of the Jordan in the form of perfect manhood, that he had imposed on the senses of his enemies, and of his disciples;

and that the ministers of Pilate had wasted their impotent rage on an airy phantom, who seemed to expire on the cross, and after three days to rise from the dead." *— Gibbon, vol. 3, chap. 21, page 320.

2. " Basilides, a man so ancient that he boasted to follow Glaucias as his master, who was the disciple of St. Peter, taught that Christ was NOT crucified ; but that a metamorphosis took place between him and Simon, the Cyrenian, who was crucified in his stead, while Jesus stood by and mocked at the mistake of the Jews. " — Pearson on the Creed, vol. 2. p. 249.

3. " Those who receive the book called the Acts, or Journeys of the Apostles PETER, JOHN, ANDREW, THOMAS, and PAUL, † must believe that Christ was not really, but only APPEARED as a man, and was seen by his disciples in various forms, sometimes as a young man, sometimes as an old man ; sometimes great, sometimes small ; sometimes so tall that his head would reach the clouds ; that he was not really crucified himself, but another in his stead, while he laughed at those who imagined that they crucified him. " — Jones on the Canon, vol. 1. p. 12.

4. The Gospel of the Helkesaites, who derived their name from Elxai or Elxæus, who lived in the time of Trajan, about A. D. 114 ; who joined himself with the Ebionites or Nazarenes, taught that Christ was a certain power, whose height was 24 schenia, or Egyptian leagues, (66 miles) and his breadth 24 miles, and his thickness proportionably wonderful. " — Jones, vol. 1. p. 226.

* Apostolis adhuc in sæculo superstitibus apud Judæam Christ anguine recente, et PHANTASMA corpus Domini asserebatur.— Sotelerious Patres Apostol. tom. 2. p. 24.

† And why should they not be received ?

Now, reader, turn to the Koran of Mahomet, the genuineness of which, no Christians have yet called in question. That is a work unquestionably of the Seventh Century, (Mahomet died, June 7th, 632;) yet, without any disparaging, decrying, or ridiculing the Christian doctrine, what it then was, and how it was understood by the writer of that holy book, appears in terms not to be mistaken.

"And the Jews devised a stratagem against him — but God devised a stratagem against them, and God is the best deviser of strategems."

With these lights in thy hand, answer to thyself, and as thou wilt—I care not, I have given thee means of answering.

1. Why — Bishop Mark should begin his Gospel with the account of Christ appearing on the banks of the Jordan, and taking no notice at all of his birth or infancy, should expressly state, that *that* was the beginning of the Gospel?

2. Why — In the reading of the three Bishops, Matthew, Mark and Luke, the insignificant, useless, and never again or any where else mentioned personage, SIMON THE CYRENIAN, should be lugged in, with no character to sustain, like a fool too many in the pantomime, having nothing to do or say in relevancy to the business of the scene?

3. Why — In the plain and grammatical construction of the text of those Bishops, as that text would be read upon a trial for murder, it should really appear that it *was* Simon the Cyrenian, who was crucified?

4. Why — That there was a real mistake or substitution of Simon, (as he is called the father of Alexander and Rufus) should be so evidently implied by Jesus himself,

in whose words addressed to Simon —Father " *(subaudi,* Father Simon !) forgive them, for they know not what they do." (Luke xxiii. 34.) These words, addressed by Jesus to Simon, are compatible with the character of a good demon, which seems to be such as the Evangelists meant to portray; they were respectful in consideration of Simon's venerable age — they were moral, as calculated to prevent or subdue the anger he might have felt against his persecutors, and they were *true* in respect of the circumstances assumed. But, applied to God they were impious, in the indecency of so familiar a style, as merely saying *Father:* they were ABSURD, as attempting to suggest a reason to infinite wisdom: and they were FALSE, in saying that the Jews knew not what they were doing; when, unless they had really got hold of the wrong person, there was no room for the possibility of a mistake in the matter !

5. Why, if Barnabas and Paul preached the same story, they should have quarrelled so bitterly, and like all other good Christians, never have been reconciled?

6. Why Paul should so emphatically say, that when he and his party preached Jesus Christ, they preached HIM crucified: if there were none, who at the same time were preaching a directly contrary doctrine — namely, Jesus Christ not crucified?—1 Corinth. i. 23.

7. Why he should call the other Apostles, false Apostles and dogs? — Philip. iii. 2. — 2 Corinth. xi. 13.

8. Why he should say that *they* preached Christ out of envy and strife? — Philip. i. 5.

9. Why he should curse them with the most bitter execrations? — 1 Corinth. xvi. 22.

10. Why he should recommend, in a sufficient hint, that they should be privately assassinated? — Gal. v. 12.

11. Why, never once in any part of the Epistles should

there be such a manner of referring to the story, as to make it seem to have been a narrative of facts?

12. Why, on every occasion that would have called for an explicit statement, or reference to facts, should the Apostles have made the most pitiful ambages, to avoid giving them?

14. Why, even the admitted first Martyr Stephen, upon the immediate freshness and then most recent occurrence of the most stupendous events that ever happened (if they ever happened) when called upon to give the grounds and reasons of his faith, should not have even glanced at the resurrection of Christ, as being any part of the grounds and reasons of his faith; nay, should not so much as have once mentioned his names, either Jesus or Christ, or led his hearers to an idea that referred to him, save in one single *conundrum* that might be riddled out with equal application to himself, or any just person that had been so unjustly treated?

14. Why in every passage where such language as would designate a real being, seems to be such as could hardly have been avoided, find we instead, the language only of mystery, trope, allegory and fiction?

15. Why, in such language as approaches nearest to a description of a real and corporal being, should the strict and literal sense, be such as cannot without impiety, absurdity and palpable contradiction be admitted — *exemplia gratia* — the Son of God, the heir of all things?

16. Why should the only line of general uniformity, in the writings of the earliest Fathers, be their concurrence in representing Jesus as a visionary hypostasis,* that had no real existence?

---

* JUSTIN MARTYR'S APOLOGY TO THE EMPEROR ADRIAN, &c.
" In saying that all things were made in this beautiful order by

17. Why should his divinity have ever been dreamed of, if his real existence, as a man, could ever have been ascertained?

God, what do we seem to say more than Plato. When we teach a general conflagration, what do we teach more than the Stoics. By opposing the worship of the works of men's hands, we concur with Menander, the comedian; and by declaring the Logos, the first begotten of God, our master Jesus Christ, to be born of a virgin, without any human mixture, to be crucified and dead, and to have rose again, and ascended into heaven: we say no more in this, than what you say of those whom you style the Sons of Jove. For you need not be told what a parcel of sons, the writers most in vogue among you, assign to Jove; there's Mercury, Jove's Interpreter, in imitation of the Logos, in worship among you. There's Æsculapius, the physician, smitten by a thunder-bolt, and after that, ascending into heaven. There's Bacchus, torn to pieces; and Hercules burnt to get rid of his pains. There's Pollux and Castor, the sons of Jove by Leda, and Perseus by Danæ; and not to mention others, I would fain know why you always deify the departed Emperors, and have a fellow at hand to make affidavit that he saw Cæsar mount to heaven from the funeral pile.

"As to the son of God, called Jesus, should we allow him to be nothing more than man, yet the title of the Son of God is very justifiable, upon the account of his wisdom, considering that you have your MERCURY in worship, under the title of the THE WORD and Messenger of God.

"As to the objection of our Jesus's being crucified, I say, that suffering was common to all the forementioned sons of Jove, but only they suffered another kind of death. As to his being born of a virgin, you have your Perseus to balance that. As to his curing the lame, and the paralytic, and such as were cripples from their birth, this is little more than what you say of you Æsculapius."—P. 76, Chapter 40.

Such were the evidences of the Christian Religion, as they were presented to the Emperor Titus Ælius Adrianus Pius Augustus Cæsar, and to his son Verissimus, and to Lucius the philosopher, by St. Justin, among the first, if not himself the very first of the Apostolic Fathers. There is hardly the difference of fifty years between this apology and St. John's Revelation. "And if the

18. Why should the greater difficulty, and consequently higher merit of faith, be made to consist in believing, that

Christian faith (says his learned translator) lived not to these years in its original purity, it came up and was cut down like a flower."— Reeve's Apologies of the Fathers, vol. 1, Lond., 1716.

It was a Catholic opinion among the philosophers, that pious frauds were good things, and that the people ought to be imposed on in matters of religion." — Ibid. p. 99.

"It was held as a maxim that it was not only lawful, but even praiseworthy to deceive, and even to use the expedient of a *lie*, in order to advance the cause of truth and piety." — Mosheim, vol. 1. p. 198.

Some of the *ancientest* writers of the church, have not scrupled to call Socrates, and some others of the best of the heathen moralists, *Christians*. — Clarke, p. 284.

2. ORIGEN'S DEFENCE OF THE CHRISTIAN RELIGION AGAINST CELSUS.

"Then Celsus, speaking of idolatry, does himself advance an argument that tends to justify and commend our practice; therefore endeavoring to show in the sequel of his discourse, that our notion of image worship was not a discovery that was owing to the Scriptures, but that we have it in common with the heathens; he quotes a passage in Heraclitus to this effect. To this I answer, that some common notions of good and evil, are originally implanted in the minds of all men; we need not wonder that Heraclitus and others whether Greeks or Barbarians, have publicly acknowledged to the world that they hold the very same notions that we maintain."— Chap. 5.

Chap. 10. — "And since our adversaries are continually making such a stir about our taking things on trust, I answer, that we who see plainly, and have found the vast advantage that the common people do manifestly and frequently reap thereby, who make up by far the greater number; I say we, who are so well advised of these things, do PROFESSEDLY teach them to believe without examination."

Such were the evidences of the Christian Religion, as they appeared to this, the very first author of a catalogue of the books contained in the New Testament. "That God should, in some extraordinary manner, visit and dwell with man, is an idea which, as we read the writings of the ancient heathens, meets us in a thousand different forms." — Bishop Horne's Discourses, vol. 3, p. 353.

he had real flesh and blood,* which no individual on earth could have doubted, had there ever existed, the least shadow of a probability, that such a man ever existed at all?

19. Why, when his divinity, as an imaginary being, (as all divinities were imaginary,) could be very well conceived; when, as a supposed personification of an abstract principle, as the Logos, or the Word, as the Genius of virtue, as Christ the power of God, or Christ the wisdom of God, poetry would allow, and philosophy would understand, the evangelical fiction; should the cannibal ceremonies of Eucharists and Sacraments,† have been devised,

---

* 1 John iv. 2. — " Every spirit that confessseth that Jesus Christ is come in the flesh, is of God."

2 John vii: — " For many deceivers are entered in the world, who confess not that Jesus Christ is come in the flesh."

1 John iv. 3. — " And every spirit that confesseth not that Jesus Christ is come in the flesh, is not of God." This is language that could not have been used, if the reality of Christ's existence as a man could not have been denied, or if the Apostle himself had been able to give any evidence whatever of the fact pretended.

" Cruci heremus, sanguinem sugimus, et inter ipsa redemptoris nostri vulnera figimus linguam," are the words of the holy Father Saint Cyprian, as quoted by Bishop Jeremy Taylor, in his Holy Living, p. 250. " We stick to the cross, we suck the blood, and loll our tongues in the very wounds of our Redeemer." It is, nevertheless, an atrocious and unfounded slander of the Mohammedans, when they call those who use this sublime and figurative language— Christian Dogs! it is evident they don't understand it.

† Cannibal Ceremony of the Sacrament — " Except ye eat of the flesh of the son of man, and drink his blood, ye have no life in you. John vi. 53. He that eateth my flesh, and drinketh my blood, dwelleth in me, and I in him ; for my flesh is meat indeed, and my blood is drink indeed." ib. 56. There can be no difficulty in admitting this to be merely figurative language ; but the difficulty is, upon such an admission, to show what sort of language it would

to subdue not merely the imaginations and the thoughts of the heart, but the perception of the senses to the obedience of faith?

20. Why, Tertullian, the first of all the Latin Fathers, Presbyter of Carthage, should reason *thus* on the evidences of Christianity? "I find no other means to prove myself to be impudent with success, and happily a fool, than by my contempt of shame; as for instance, I maintain that the Son of God was born; why am I not ashamed of maintaining such a thing? Why! but because it is itself a shameful thing. — I maintain that the Son of God died; well, *that* is wholly credible, because it is monstrously absurd. — I maintain, that after having been buried, he rose again; and *that* I take to be absolutely true, because it was manifestly impossible." Excellent faith! as the Doctor will not give me credit even for ability to give a literal translation, I offer the above only as a bold guess;* below is the text itself, and he may get his Grammar and Dictionary and mend it.

21. And why, there is no power of language — no use of words — no modes of expression and significancy, that could possibly have been used to express and signify a real and corporeal presence, that are not and have not,

---

be, that was *not* figurative. It is not to be wondered at, that when our Christian Missionaries preach this sort of mysticism to the Anthropophagies, Caffrees, Carribees, and Catabanks, they should be listened to with the profoundest attention; their hearers would whet their knives; the Chickasaws, the Choctaws, and the Cherokees, would *squeal* with rapture.

* Alias non invenio materias confusionis, quæ me per contemptum ruboris probent, bene impudentem et feliciter stultum. Natus est Dei filius non pudet, quia pudendum est: Et mortuus est Dei filius, prorsus credibile est, quia ineptum est. Et sepultus, resurrexit, certum est quia impossibile." — De Carne Christi, Semler's Edition Halæ Magdeburgicæ, 1770. Vol. 3, p. 352.

from the earliest ages of the church, been used in shameless prostitution to the maintenance of *that* as true, which every sense and faculty of man did at the same time show to be false.

The divinity of Christ was comprehensible by men's imaginations — his humanity, the flesh and blood, stuck in their teeth.

Innumerable other passages there are, in these mystical and mischievous writings, in confirmation of the irrefutable truth of the Manifesto, and in abundant supply of SCRIPTURE-EVIDENCE, that the " blessed Jesus " never existed.

Of these there are so many, that they may be safely left to the reader's own observance; and if he should say that he really cannot find them out; all I have to say is, no more can I! I could not show St. Paul's cathedral to the man who stood on Ludgate-hill, and had bound himself by vow to look only towards Temple-bar.

Nor do I pretend to have offered any thing in the shape of an argument, or in the least degree to have refuted the Answer to the Manifesto, in the judgment of any reader, who shall think for himself, — provided only that he shall do so SERIOUSLY and DEVOUTLY, and above all, with PRAYERS — with prayers to the SUPREME AUTHOR OF TRUTH, upon the truly modest and humble assumption, that the Supreme Author of Truth must be just exactly of the same way of thinking as himself. The reader must only give heed to the admonitions laid before him so pastorally, so ministerially, and so judiciously, by the learned and pious Doctor; he must take care not to violate his duty as a Christian, and not to be wise above what Dr. John Pye Smith has written for the strengthening of his faith, and for the building up, not only of his understanding, but also of his disposition and temper, into a holy conformity to that mind which was also in Christ Jesus; and then, he will not only see that all passages purporting to be quotations in the Manifesto, and in this Vindication of it, are " impudent forgeries, and that the passages referred to say no such thing as is imputed to them;" but he will also feel that " the Manifesto Writer is the first-born of calumny — the greatest liar that ever set pen to paper," &c., &c., &c., and that the wisdom and justice of our laws cannot be too much applauded, for having cut off such a pest from society, and assigned him to the highly merited horrors of solitary confinement.

But as the Doctor, though he so earnestly recommends the use of prayer, has not drawn up a form proper and suitable for the imploring of such a right understanding, and such a heavenly frame of mind, I take the liberty, as having myself, for many years, been a laborer in the vineyard, to supply his lack of service.

PRAYER,

To be said by the readers of John Pye Smith's Answer to the Manifesto, first having thrown this Vindication into the fire, and then devoutly kneeling, for the greater self-abasement and humbling of their proud reason before God :—

O Lord God! Father of our Lord Jesus Christ, and *Supreme Author of Truth!* thou knowest that the carnal mind is enmity itself, against thee, and against thy dearly beloved Son — thou knowest that man, in his natural estate, and exercising only his rational faculties, perceiveth not the things that belong to the Spirit, and that they are foolishness to him; as I confess, O Lord, that when I use my reason, they also appear to be to me; wherefore, I beseech thee, watch and guard over that dangerous and betraying faculty, and grant, that whenever my reason says one thing, my faith may be ready to say another. Save me, O Lord! above all things, I beseech thee, from the craft and subtlety of the devil, who at this time has, by thy allowance, been permitted to assail thy church with sore and grievous temptations, and who has raised up and inspired such a devilish minister of sin, who was once seemingly a minister of grace, and so endowed him with his hellish and infernal gifts, that by his means he not only denies the Lord Jesus Christ, but even denies! — O Lord! O Lord! he denies every thing, — Forgive me, O God! for ever having looked into his book, or trusted my weak faith to look on one of his accursed arguments. " Persecute him, O Lord! with thy tempests and vex him with thy storms ; pour out thine indignation upon him, and let thy wrathful displeasure take hold of him. Let death come hastily upon him, and let him go down quick into hell." *(Psalm. Psalm, Psalm.)* And O Lord! I beseech thee, take away from me the understanding that would understand any thing that is not in harmony with thy word. Make me to see that which I see not, and to understand that which I cannot understand. Make me to feel assured that *that* is certainly false which my reason, without thy especial interference, would as certainly pronounce to be true. Make the things to *be*, which are not: and enable me, after the example of thy holy servant, John Pye Smith, to call every thing forgery and falsehood, that tends to bring thy holy word into doubt and uncertainty — like him, may I have courage to defend myself — to forswear the use of my own eyes — to see not what I do see, and to see what I do not. Like him, O God! may I always, when by thy help I have gained a victory over my carnal convictions, refused the evidence of my own senses, and set my own reason at defiance ; then may I attack infidels in thy strength, O Lord! and be exceeding bold in thy salvation — then may I apply to them those names of scorn and infamy which would be due to myself, were I not thy servant, and did not my lies abound to thy glory, through Jesus Christ, our Lord. Amen.

APPENDIX.

THE GREAT DIFFICULTY FAIRLY STATED.

WE have shown the main story, and all the leading doctrines of Christianity, to have existed in the world many ages before the period which Christianity assigns as that of their first promulgation. Yet we charge the writings of the New Testament, in which that story, and those doctrines are exhibited, as betraying internal marks of an origin, *modern*, even in relation to that assigned period.

Here is indeed a great difficulty. No candid Christian can deny that the New Testament contains innumerable passages, which can by no possibility be conceived to have been written, either *in*, or any thing like to *near*, the times to which they refer. No candid unbeliever can deny that it also contains innumerable passages, and a general sketch most clearly to be recognized, entirely *up* to the times, and *in* and *at* the times supposed.

The passage which I here subjoin, from IRENÆUS, the first of all the Fathers who has mentioned the names of the four Evangelists, is, I sincerely believe, the very strongest testimony in favor of the Christian Evidences that I have ever met with. If the Christians, who seem generally to have held dexterity in forging the highest Christian accomplishment, have not forged this, or perhaps substituted the names of Matthew, Mark, Luke, and John, for those which they found in the passage itself.

"Such is the certain truth of our Gospels, that the heretics themselves bear testimony to them, every one of them endeavoring to prove his particular doctrines from thence. But the Ebionites may be refuted from the Gospel of Matthew, which alone they receive. Marcion useth only the Gospel of LUKE, and that mutilated; nevertheless, from what he retains, it may be shown, that he blasphemes the one only God. They who divide Jesus from Christ, and say that Christ always remained impassible, whilst Jesus suffered; prefer the Gospel of MARK. However, if they read with a love of truth, they may thence be convinced of their error. The Valentinians receive the Gospel of JOHN, entire, in order to prove their pairs of Æons; and by that gospel they may be confuted. Since therefore, persons of different persuasions agree with us in making use of this testimony, our evidence for the authority of these Gospels is certain and unquestionable." Thus translated from the Latin of the Greek, by Lardner, vol. 4, p. 521. In the excellent theological library of a gentleman, whom 'tis the proudest and happiest feeling of my heart to call my friend, I have collated the original text, which Lardner seems to have wanted for this passage.

THE SOLUTION OF THE DIFFICULTY.

This driving up to the mark, drives beyond it. If we believe the Fathers, we must believe them throughout. The very high antiquity of Irenæus, as the disciple of Papias, the disciple of St. John, proves the still higher antiquity of the various orders of heretics, whom he undertakes to refute; they must have been established; their tenets must have been extensively diffused. The Gospels therefore, on which they founded their various systems, had obtained authority and prevalence, long, very long, before the time which should suit with them; and however modified, castigated, and ascribed to other authorities, were really PAGAN in their origin, and were brought in by the Gnostics, Valentinians, Essenes, Therapeutæ, and various other itinerant adventurers and travelling philosophers, from the sacred legends of the Hindoo, Phœnician, and Grecian mythologies.

If we believe the testimony of the Fathers, we must abide the conclusions to which they conduct us; yet one and all, from Tertullian in the second, to Lactantius in the fourth century, quote as genuine, those Sibylline verses which related the whole story of Christ's incarnation, death resurrection, and miracles, to Tarquinius Priscus, 717 years before Christ, almost in the very words of the Gospels. These verses according to Bishop Pearson, actually exhibited an anagram of the whole Christian Mythology, in the mystical word $IX\Theta Y\Sigma$, a fish, the letters of which stand for $I\eta\sigma\?\varsigma\ X\varrho\iota\sigma\tau o\varsigma\ \Theta\epsilon\?\ Y\iota o\varsigma\ \Sigma\omega\tau\eta\varrho$, Jesus Christ, the Son of God — the Savior; and the Christian Sozomen was strengthened in his faith by the authority of that Pagan Hexameter.

Ω ξυλον, ω μακαριστον 'εφ ᾧ Θεος εξετανυσθη.
O wood, most blessed! upon which God was stretched!*

There can be no doubt, that had the objections of Porphyry, Hierocles, Celsus, and other enemies of the Christian faith been permitted to come down to us, the *plagiarism* of the Christian scriptures from previously existing Pagan documents, is the specific charge that would have been brought against them. But these, as we have seen, were ordered to be burned, by the prudent piety of the Christian emperors. In writings which, like those of Victor, (see page 51,) have by happy accident, escaped the expunging policy of Christians, or incidental passages whose significancy has eluded their observance, in those which they have suffered to come down to us, will be found the neuclus of truth, *e. g.* There is a passage in Cicero, written forty years before the birth of Christ, in which he ridicules the doctrine of transubstantiation, and asks how a man can be so stupid as to imagine that which he eats to be a God? " Ut illud quo vascatur Deum esse putet." Never should it be forgotten, that we have only been allowed to know what the objections of Celsus were, per favor of such extracts from his writings as his opponent, Origen, found it convenient to answer; and if Origen were the author of the objections, as well as of the answers to them, he would not have been the first Christian Jack-o'-both-sides.

---

* See also how the Christian Father Minucius Felix, taunts the Pagans — " You it is, ye Pagans, who worship a cross with a man upon it!" What desperate fools those Pagans must have been to worship a crucified ——.

It wouldn't have done to have suffered Celsus to ask him to show proof of the existence of Christ as a man, to have called on him to produce a copy of the register of his crucifixion, or to refer to any extraneous and independent evidence.

The dissimulations practiced by Ebionite Christians, in order to fabricate evidence for the existence of Christ, as a man, against the Nazarene, Docetian, and Phantasmiastic Christians, who universally maintained that he was a ghost, and that every thing related of him occurred only in vision, are absolutely immeasurable. Every testimony of this kind hitherto produced, has turned out, upon thorough investigation, to be a most flagrant forgery. Addison was deceitful, or deceived enough to profess a belief in the letter of Christ to Abgarus; and Macknight and Doddridge have been gulled, or have attempted to gull others into a belief, that the gods and dæmons had borne testimony to their blessed Saviour: upon the authority of the admissions of Porphyry, in his "*Philosophy of Oracles*," which admissions of Porphyry, Porphyry never made — but the whole work was the forgery of Christian hands for the purpose of making him *seem* to have made such admissions. — *Lardner, in loco.*

Even Lardner himself was not honest, where he found that honesty and the pretence of evidence for Christianity were incompatible. He could represent the Emperor Julian as a persecutor, in direct despite of historical fact, merely because Julian was not a Christian; yet tells us of Constantine, after he had murdered — 1. Maximian, his wife's father; 2. Bassianus, husband of his sister Anastasia; 3. Licinius, husband of his sister Constantia; 4. Licinianus, his nephew; 5. Fausta, his wife, and 6 Crispus his son — that " he was a sincere Christian, and neither a cruel prince, nor a bad man." Zosimus had given the most rational account of his conversion,* and Sozomen, in refutation, admits the report that Constantine. having put to death some of his relations, and particularly his son Crispus, and being sorry for what he had done, applied to Sopater the philosopher; and he answering that there were no expiations for such offences: the Emperor then had recourse to the Christian Bishops, who told him that by repentance and baptism he might be cleansed from all sin; with which doctrine he was mightily pleased. Whereupon he became a Christian himself, and required his subjects to be so likewise.† — Quoted by Lardner, vol. 4, p. 400.

It is well known, that the whole of Ecclesiastical History must stand or fall with the character of its great pillar, EUSEBIUS. Well, Lardner, after making admissions with respect to this great Father of Christianity, little calculated to strengthen any man's faith, stumbles at last upon the very door that would let out *every thing* — but bangs it in our faces, and is gone — 'tis the blue chamber — the truth is there!! But here's a peep through the key-hole,

" It is *wonderful*, that Eusebius should think Philo's THERAPEUTÆ were Christians, and that their ANCIENT

---

* See page 42.

† Ταυτα συν επισταμενος εαυτω, και προςετιγε ορκων καταφρονησεις, προσηει τοις ιερευσι καθαρσια σιτων. Και τοτο εχειν επαγγελμα το τας ασεβεις μεταγαμζατοντας αυτης πασης αμαρτιας εξω παρακρημα καθιστασθαι. So far Lardner gives us the text of Zosimus.

Αδημονεντα δε τον Βασιγεα επι τη απαγορευσει, περιτυχειν Επισκοποις, οι μετανοια και Βαπτισματι υπεσχοντο, πασης αυτον αμαρτιας καθαιρειν. Sozomen in loco eodem. This is not the language of ridicule, their own most sacred compositions will furnish stronger satire.

WRITINGS WERE OUR GOSPELS AND EPISTLES !!!" — Vol. 2, p. 461. No! it is not wonderful that he should *think* so — the wonder is that he should have *said so*. A hundred thousand volumes are contained in that saying's sense!

It should be steadily borne in remembrance, that the terms CHRIST; CHRIST OUR SAVIOUR; OUR LORD: OUR BLESSED LORD AND SAVIOUR: are epithets that have no indentification in them. They were of familiar application, and in continual recurrence as applied to the Sun, to Jupiter, to Bacchus, Apollo, Adonis, &c.; in the multifarious systems of Heliolatry and Idolatry, that had for antecedent ages of ages, subjugated the abused reason of mankind.

By application of this essential canon of criticism, some of the earliest pretended testimonies to OUR LORD, and to OUR SAVIOUR, will be found to have more probably referred to some one or other of those Pagan Deities. Thus, the very earliest, that of the Apology of QUADRATUS, pretended to have been presented to Adrian, in the year 126, in which he tells the Emperor, that " the works of our Saviour were always conspicuous, for they were real; both they that were healed, and they that were raised from the dead, who were seen not only when they were healed, or raised, but for a long time afterwards, not only whilst he dwelled on this earth, but also after his departure, and for a good while after it, insomuch that some of them have reached to our times;"* has no distinctiveness of

---

* I subjoin the whole of this precious fragment; it is impossible that it could have been presented in this state to the Emperor. It is but a broken sentence; and no reason can be conceived why, having thus much of it, we should not have had more, but that the crafty Eusebius, on whose fidelity it rests was aware that its context and connexion would have betrayed its Pagan origination :—

Christian significancy. Such testimony, coming from a priest of Æsculapius, as, for all that appears, this Quadratus may have been, contains nothing but what such a priest would have said of such a deity. It hath no more indication of reference to a Jesus of Nazareth in particular, than to a Guy of Warwick.

The idolatrous epithet, CHRIST; in one of the Pagan Gospels of the ancient sect of the THERAPEUTÆ, which Gospels, as we have seen, Eusebius thinks were the same as ours,* gave great offence to the Therapeutan Thaumaturg, who, when one of his satellites had called him " the Christ of God, straitly charged and commanded them to tell no man that thing." Luke ix. 21.

The complimentary epithet, CHREST, (from which, by what is called the Iotacism, or change of the long E into I, a term of respect grew into one of worship,) signified nothing more than a good man. Clemens Alexandrinus, in the second century, founds a serious argument on this paronomasia, that,† all who believed in *Chrest*, (*i. e.* in a good man,) both are, and are called *Chrestians*, that is, good men. — Strommata, b. 2,

---

Τȣ δε Σωτηρος ημων τα εργα, αει παρην, αληθη γαρ ην οι θεραπευθεντες, οι αναστάντες εκ νεκρων οι ȣκ ωφθησαν μονον θεραπευομενοι και αναστάμενοι, αλλα και αει παρόντες, ȣδε επιδημȣντος μονον τȣ σωτηρος, αλλα και απαλλαγεντος, ησαν επι χρονον ικανον, ωστε και εις τȣς ημετερȣς τινες αυτων αφικοντο.

Thus, with no address, no connection, no purport, no conclusion; what can we infer from the existence of such a fragment and no more, but that there might not have been another sentence in the document, but what would have shown its pagan character, and so have defeated the use for which it had been *stolen*.

* Αυτικα οι εις χριστον πεπιστευκοτες χρηστοι τε εισι και λεγονται. — Strom.

† Lib. 3, c. 17, p. 53, et circa. — Psal. 55, D.

APPENDIX.

It has been the universal trick of the Christian evangelizers, to plagiarise and adopt Pagan documents, and *christen* them into Gospels: and to give a Christian *turn of the matter*, to an unquestionably idolatrous phraseology. I wish I never found the important additament, JESUS CHRIST, in Lardner's English text, where I could read no further than ο κυριος και σωτηρ ημον, *our Lord and Saviour*, in his Greek originals; a formulary as idiomatically heathenish, as Ζες μεγιστε κυδιστε κελαινεφες αιθερι ναιων in Homer's Iliad.

So hungry, however, was this great Christian Evidence manufacturer, to find testimonies to Christ and Christianity, or anything that could be strained, no matter with how much straining, into a possible reference to it, that he actually quotes the Metamorphoses of Apuleius, of Madaura, an avowed work of imagination, and brings in a Jack Ass, as bearing testimony to Christ, where the dumb beast is representing the character of a baker's wife, to whom he had been sold, and of whom he says, that* "she so abused her husband, that even he (the Ass,) could not but lament his unhappy condition; she had every vice without any thing that was agreeable. She was perverse, ill-natured, obstinate, given to drink, she robbed her husband, was profuse in her expenses; deceiving all men, especially her miserable husband, and devoting herself to

---

* " Ut, Hercules! ego, ejus vicem quoque tacitus frequenter ingemiscerem : nec ullum vitium nequissimæ illi feminæ deerat. Scæva, Sæve, vitiosa, ebriosa, pervicax, pertinax, in rapinis turpibus avara, in sumptibus turpis, profusa, inimica fidei, shostis pudicitiæ, fallens omnes homines, et miserum maritum decipiens, matutino mero, et continuo stupro corpus maniciparat — Spretis atque calcatis divinis numinibus, in vicem certæ religionis mentita sacrilega, præsumptione Dei, quem prædicaret unicum." — Apuleius, A. D. 164, more fully than above.

drinking, and .... from morning to night." And upon this description, and a little more of it, to the like effect, Lardner concludes with the words, " there can be no doubt that Apuleius here designs to represent a Christian woman!" — Vol. 4, p. 107.

It is something worse than this compliment to the ladies; when in order to make the Platonic philosopher Amelius, (A. D. 263,) seem to recognize Christ's real existence as a man, he gives an Ebionitish rendering to his Docetian Original, and so makes Amelius seem to say, that Christ took the form of a man, (vol. 4, p. 200,) instead of saying, (which was all his sense implies,) that he was the Phantasmagora* of a man.

A regular succession of the most learned and intelligent of the Christian Fathers, from and in the Apostolic age, steadily maintained, that Christ never had any real existence as a man; that he was merely a phantom or hobgoblin, and that all the business of his crucifixion and miracles took place only in a vision. These, from the Greek word, which expresses their sentiment, are called the Docetæ, or Docetian Fathers, as opposed to the Ebionite, or Beggar Heretics, who maintained the contrary hypothesis, that Jesus had a real existence. The previous prevalence of these conflicting opinions may be discerned even in the present garbled and transmuted text of our New Testament.

"Remember that Jesus Christ, of the seed of David, was raised from the dead *according to my Gospel*," 2 Timothy, ii. 8. A memorandum that can hardly be conceived to have been sent to a Christian bishop, unless there were some other Gospels in being at that time, which told the

---

* Ηξιωσε την μεϱφην ανθϱωπε λαβειν, were the words which Amelius would have used, had he meant as Dr. Lardner renders him; but φαντασεσθαι, ανθϱωπον is the text; which is rather awkward.

story in a different way. The three Evangelists, Matthew Mark and Luke, distinctly relate one of Christ's Metamorphoses, and the words of John xii. 28, " Father, CLARIFY thy name! then came there a voice from heaven, saying, I have both clarified it, and I will clarify it again;"* are words that could not possibly have been written by one who wished to be understood otherwise than as *romancing*. Would any sensible man look another in the face, and say he believed it?

The doctrine of Leucius or Lucian, (A. D. 143,) who by arguments more and more cogent than my limits would allow me to touch on, may be shown to be the author of the Received Gospel, according to Saint Luke, and of the Acts of the Apostles, was,† " that Christ was not truly a man, but in appearance only, and that he appeared to his disciples in different forms, at different times, sometimes young, and then as an old man, and then again as a boy, sometimes greater, then less, then greater than ever, so that his head would reach the midst of heaven, and that Christ was not crucified, but another in his stead."

His boyish character, however, seems on all hands, to be admitted as that " *on which wise*," he made his last appearance, as we find the Apostles speaking of him, as

---

* CLARIFY is the real original word in our native tongue, which has had both its sound and sense, spouted away in the more sonorous but insignificant mouthing of it into *glorify*. The oldest Latin copies in existence, enriched our language with this word, John xxi. 19, stood, " Hoc autem dixit significans qua morte clarificaturus esset Deum, " — by what death he should CLARIFY God.

† Λεγει δε μηδ' ανθρωπησαι αγηθως τον χριστον αλλα δοξαι, και ιτελλα πολλακις φανηναι τοις μαθηταις, νεον και πρεσβυτην παλιν, και παλιν παιδα, και, μειζονα, και ελαττονα, και μεγιστον ποτε την κορυφην διηκειν εσθ' οτι μεχοι ουρσυ ; και τον χριστον μη σταυρωθηναι αλλ' ετεροον αντ' αυτου.

of that fashion, after his Apotheosis; "thy holy boy Jesus," Acts iv. 27. "That signs and wonders may be done by the name of thy holy boy Jesus." Acts iv. 30. To be sure, those words savor somewhat of the ancient Liturgy of the jolly God Bacchus, ever fair and young; but the smaller compass his body could be reduced into, the more convenient it would be for ascending into "the clouds of heaven, with power and great *clary*."

It should however, never be forgotten, that those who opposed the Docetian doctrines, and maintained the extraordinary notion of an historical foundation of the Gospel-Theophany, and that Jesus Christ was really a man, have failed in every attempt that they have made to adduce independent testimony. In order to be able to pretend that the adversaries of Christianity had *admitted* the real existence of Jesus Christ as a man, they actually wrote books themselves for those adversaries, forging upon them, and so fathering them with admissions that they never did, and never would have admitted.

Celsus, in all probability, never so much as saw the work which the mendacious Origen has won immortal fame by affecting to refute. He never would have made so foolish an admission as "that Christ wrought real miracles by the power of magic," which Origen could so easily answer: nor would he have failed of asking a question or two which Origen would have found to be answered not quite so easily.*

---

* Even at this day, we find the advocates of Christianity relying on the real cruelty and affected contempt with which they can treat their adversaries — " Did Origen represent Jesus Christ as the hero of a fable?" asks Mr. Beard, "You are challenged to the proof of it," (Letter I. to Mr. Carlile.) Would Mr. Beard only turn to the 27th Chapter of Origen's Answer to Celsus, he would find that

APPENDIX. 189

In the three books of the philosophy of Oracles,* so fraudulently ascribed to PORPHYRY, the most virtuous and formidable enemy of the Christian craft, even the GOD APOLLO is represented as having recognized the existence of Jesus Christ as a virtuous and religious man. This egregious cheat was not too gross to be held out by Eusebius in his challange to the Pagans. The great pillar of Ecclesiastical history and of priestcraft, could thus conceal the consciousness of imposture under pomp and parade of declamations.

" But thou," (as if addressing Porphyry, or some one who had made the admissions ascribed to Porphyry)† " But thou, at least, listen to thine own gods, to thy oracular deities themselves, who have borne witness and ascribed to our Saviour not imposture, as thou dost, but piety and wisdom, and ascension into heaven."

The orthodox Ignatius, never alludes to the actions and sufferings of Christ without sufficient intimation that his whole history had in it enough of " the stuff that dreams are made of." " His incarnation, death, and resurrection, three of the mysteries most spoken of in the world, were hidden from human observance, and done in secret by God."‡ Every attempt to bolster them into credibility as facts, has failed.—

Origen has described the crucifixion as a scene in a *tragedy*,—to his 7th Chapter, he would find that he acknowledged, that the name IESUS, was only a sacred *spell*,—in Chapter 10th, that Christianity would never bear examining. For a Unitarian to quote Origen, is downright bravoism !

* Περι της εκ λογιων φιλοσφιας.

† Αλλα συγε, καν των σαυτε δαιμονων, αυτων δη των χρησμωδων θεων ακες, τω σωτηρι ημων ϫ' ωσπερ ου γοητειαν. αλλα Ευσεβειαν, και σοφιαν, και εις ερανες ανοδον μαρτυρεντων.—Dem. Ev. l. 3. chap. 6.

‡ Quoted, as I remember.

The pretended letter of Pilate to Tiberius;
The correspondence of Christ and Abgarus;
The once famous Sibylline Verses;
The testimony of Phlegon;
The Admissions of Porphyry;
The celebrated passage of Josephus;
once constituting the redoubtable array of the evidences of the Christian Religion, have one by one been beaten off the ground, or surrendered by Christians themselves as no longer tenable. Not one single document is there of the existence of Christ as a man, within the first hundred years. What can we say of a religion that hath no better evidence than this, but that it hath every mark of imposture upon it, that imposture could possibly be conceived to have. Chronology puts out all her lights to hide the blushes of history at the mention of it.

CONCLUSION.

As we see Protestantism to be a mere modification or reform of Popery, so Popery was nothing more than a similar modification or reform of Paganism.* It is absolutely certain that the Pagans were in possession of the whole Gospel story many ages before its Jewish origen was pretended; and it was not till the first error had been committed,

---

* The Fathers make no scruple of admitting this, with respect to all the dissenting forms of Christianity — " εκ γαρ ελγηνικων μυθων πασαι αι αιρεσεις," says Ephiphanias — " All the heresies were derived from the Greek fables, " that is, in other words, there is cheating in every trade but ours.

of suffering the people to become acquainted too intimately with the contents of the sacred books, that it became necessary to invent a chronology, and to give to "airy nothing a local habitation and a name." The advance of the human mind has beaten away, even these last refuges of imposture, and in the absence of all hope of ever being able to set up grounds of rational evidence again, Christianity rests her dying struggle on the fanaticism of the vulgar, and the craft of the informed — the willingness to be deceived on the part of the many, and the power to punish those who would undeceive them, in the hands of the mighty.

When "honor, wealth, and power unlimited," incite and reward the machinations of hypocrisy, and penalties and pains are the meed of honesty and truth, the balance of chances is somewhat too much against the hope of struggling virtue. It is hardly to be expected, but that when danger and disgrace attend the avowal of their better knowledge, the better knowing will keep that knowledge to themselves. Thus audacious ignorance tramples on modest truth — craft makes sure of the neutrality of prudence — the multitude believe, and impostors triumph. The voice of boisterous fanaticism rings in her gorgeous temples — the remonstrance of persecuted reason is put forth from the cells of captivity.

ROBERT TAYLOR.

England, Oakham Gaol, May, 1828.

CPSIA information can be obtained at www.ICGtesting.com
Printed in the USA
LVOW04s0035120515

438054LV00038B/2770/P